D0146717

The Word and the Cross

The Word and the Cross

STANISLAS BRETON

Translated with an introduction by
JACQUELYN PORTER

Fordham University Press
New York
2002

ARMY TRACES A CATHOLIC LIBRARY
1100 EAST 55TH STREET
CHICAGO, ILLINOIS 60615

BT
453
.B7413
2002

Introduction and translation copyright © 2002 by Fordham University Press
Originally published as *Le verbe et la croix* in Paris in 1981. © 1981 – Desclée

All rights reserved. No part of this publication may be reproduced, stored in
a retrieval system, or transmitted in any form or by any means—electronic,
mechanical, photocopy, recording, or any other—except for brief quotations
in printed reviews, without the prior permission of the publisher.

"Being, God and the Poetics of Relation" reprinted from *Dialogues with Contemporary Continental Thinkers,* edited by Richard Kearney (Manchester
University Press, 1984). Reprinted by permission of Richard Kearney.

Perspectives in Continental Philosophy, No. 22
ISSN 1089–3938

Library of Congress Cataloging-in-Publication Data

Breton, Stanislas.
    [Verbe et la croix. English]
    The Word and the Cross / Stanislas Breton ; translated with an
introduction by Jacquelyn Porter.—1st ed.
        p.   cm.—(Perspectives in continental philosophy ; no. 22)
    Includes bibliographical references and index.
    ISBN 0-8232-2157-1 (hardcover)—ISBN 0-8232-2158-X (pbk.)
    1. Jesus Christ—Crucifixion. 2. Logos (Christian theology)   I.
Title.   II. Series
    BT453 .B7413   2002
    230'.2—dc21
                                            2001040641

Printed in the United States of America
02 03 04 05 06 5 4 3 2 1
First Edition

JESUIT - KRAUSS - McCORMICK - LIBRARY
1100 EAST 55th STREET
CHICAGO, ILLINOIS 60615

CONTENTS

TRANSLATOR'S INTRODUCTION

In 1981, Stanislas Breton published *The Word and the Cross*,[1] a brief but startlingly original work that became a small spiritual classic. Although the author had written extensively in philosophy, this work, perhaps because of its "half-philosophic and half-theological" genre,[2] impressed a wider audience. Like a late sketch of a master artist, it distills a lifetime's thought and meditation. Yet the work defies classification in terms typical of French postmodern thought. It draws from a controversial lexicon key terms such as origin, logos, and Being, implicated by some of Breton's colleagues and contemporaries in their critiques of onto-theology and logocentrism. Breton, however, radicalizes these terms, rethinking them to resist all forms of triumphalism and exclusivity. The work insists upon the mind's need for unity and alludes to the schemas of Thomism and Neoplatonism. Yet it also celebrates forgotten mystics and the decentering enactments of "the fools of Christ." The author himself was a paradox on the Parisian intellectual scene. Rooted in his own Catholic tradition, he nonetheless shared a post at the Ecole normale supérieure with Louis Althusser and Jacques Derrida. While he has passed leisure time tilling monastery gardens, he has been described at the same time in conversations with Foucault and Althusser in the latter's cell.[3]

These paradoxes suggest that *The Word and the Cross* needs to be read in relation to Breton's larger philosophical project.

---

[1] Stanislas Breton, *Unicité et monothéisme* (Paris: Cerf, 1981).

[2] Paul Ricoeur, "Logos, Mythos, Stauros," in *Philosopher par passion et par raison. Stanislas Breton,* ed. Luce Giard (Grenoble: Jérome Millon, 1990), 125.

[3] Louis Althusser, *The Future Lasts Forever,* translated by Richard Veasey (New York: The New Press, 1993), 270–73.

This introduction aims to provide an overview of Breton's thought that will help readers unfamiliar with his work to see its continuity with the questions that guided him. It does not attempt a comprehensive treatment of his extensive corpus, nor can it summarize his intricately wrought investigations. It will situate some major works in the context of his life and then look more closely at the distinctive contributions of *The Word and the Cross*, a work of a somewhat different order.

ITINERARY

Breton was born in the Gironde area of France in 1912 and was orphaned at an early age. Raised by the elder of his sisters, he developed an appreciation for rural life. At the age of fifteen, he entered a Roman Catholic seminary of the Passionist order, whose spirituality centered on the Cross.[4] He claims that he never lost his appreciation for the vitality of the concretely experienced world, especially that of his early years in the Vendée region. Even though his early studies were scholastic, he was able to retain in this formative period a dual passion for philosophy and poetry. In his Thomistic studies, he was drawn to the intellectual precision and architectural symmetry of the Summas as well as to the way in which his professors used the Latin language to explicate them. The distinctions they made with the prepositions *in, de,* and so forth, opened up the medieval treatises to him as worlds of dynamic relations. He would pursue his early interest in language and the philosophy of relations through the study of phenomenology. Yet he remained appreciative of Thomism because of its intellectual rigor and clarity in defining positions. His Thomistic studies convinced him of an exigency of the mind for unity that he would retain despite his later sympathy with philosophers of dissonance.

Before completing his studies, Breton was sent by his order to a Passionist house in Rome, where he studied at the Angel-

---

[4] See Stanislas Breton, *De Rome À Paris: Itinéraire philosophique* (Desclée de Brouwer, 1992); see also Jacquelyn Porter, "Stanislas Breton's Use of Neoplatonism to Interpret the Cross in a Postmodern Setting," *The Heythrop Journal* 39 (July 1998): 264–79, in which much of this biographical research first appeared.

icum. His studies, however, were interrupted by the Second World War when, in 1939, three years after ordination, he was mobilized into the infantry. Captured by the Germans in 1940, he was sent to Austria and spent five years in a prison camp, the environment of which allowed some mental stimulus and permitted him and the diverse group of soldiers, Jews, and Serbs to engage in a study program. With the aid of a few texts of Brunschvicq, Hamelin, and Bochenski that he had carried with him,[5] he began to write a dissertation concerning the metaphysics of relations. Early in 1945, as the Russians bombed Austria, Breton despaired of rescue and threw his dissertation into the Danube River. He and other prisoners survived the bombing and were liberated by the American army, but the experience of terror affected his equilibrium and motor functions, requiring a long period of recuperation. In these ten years he turned increasingly to mystical writings such as those of Eckhart and to more obscure and discordant figures of the tradition, such as the Jesuit mystic and exorcist Surin and the "fools of Christ."

After his return to France Breton was sent to Rome where he completed a dissertation in the required Aristotelian-Thomist framework, *L'Esse in et l'esse ad dans la métapysique de l'être*.[6] Thomas had used the Aristotelian terms "being in" *(esse in)* and "being toward" *(esse ad)* to show how relations might subsist in God (the *esse in* aspect), while allowing for a Trinity of persons. The *esse ad,* which Thomas once described as a *transitio,* or a certain passage,[7] recalled for Breton the biblical emphasis upon dispossession and exodus. It suggested to him, as he remarked in an interview, that "God as a Being-in-itself, as an ideal substance, cannot be thought by us; we can only know or speak about God in terms of His relation to us or ours to Him."[8] A

---

[5] L. Brunschvicq, *La modalité du jugement*; O. Hamelin, *L'essai sur les elements principaux de la représentation*; I. J. Bochenski, *Elementi di Logica Symbolica.*

[6] Stanislas Breton, *L'Esse in et l'esse ad dans la métapysique de l'être* (Rome: Pontifical University of the Propaganda, 1951).

[7] Stanislas Breton, *Etre, Monde et Imaginaire* (Paris: Le Seuil, 1976), 268.

[8] Richard Kearney, "Being, God and the Poetics of Relation," in *States of Mind: Dialogues with Contemporary Thinkers* (New York: New York University Press, 1995), 246–261. Kearney's interview with Breton has been reprinted in the appendix to the present edition.

tendency to privilege function over substance led some professors to point to a tendency toward idealism in his work, but he was asked on the basis of it to teach at the Pontifical University of the Propaganda. In a Rome characterized by a doctrinal vigilance, he was nonetheless able to study Nietzsche, Husserl, Marx, Lenin, and Feuerbach and pursue an interest in mathematics. Though he would continue to regard Thomism as the "paleoencephalus" of his thought, he abandoned the use of Thomism as a foundation, convinced that the master himself would have preferred to inspire innovation. Breton reflected especially on the notion of the *esse ad* that symbolized for him intentionality and existence. During this golden age of Husserl he sought to explore these themes through phenomenology rather than through Thomistic metaphysics.

Conscience et intentionalité, (1956)[9] and *Approches phéno-menologique de l'idée d'être* (1959)[10] are characteristic of this early phase of his phenomenological inquiries[11] and later became the basis of a thesis for a French state doctorate read by Paul Ricoeur. In *Conscience et intentionalité*, Breton attempted to discern and describe psychological, functional, and transcendent levels in Thomistic texts. He was less interested in phenomenological reduction than in the way in which phenomenology opened up a means of inquiring, at the transcendent level, into the idea of Being and its function. The Being of ontologies, he found, tended at that time to be assimilated reductively into the notion of the possible as presented in the philosophy of Leibniz and the theologies that preceded him. He preferred to analyze Being according to a hierarchy of functions, which he called the synthetic, that which composes denominations; the positional, or that which posits determinations in a sphere of Being; and the doxic, the taking of a position through affirmation or denial. In this analysis, Breton recognized the complexity of the levels in which Being finds expres-

---

[9] Stanislas Breton, *Conscience et intentionalité* (Paris et Lyon: Vitte, 1956).
[10] Stanislas Breton, *Situation de la philosophie contemporaine* (Paris et Lyon: Vitte, 1959).
[11] See Stanislas Breton, "Postface," in *Foi et raison logique* (Paris: Le Seuil, 1971), 267–81.

sion. He sought further to root Being in act *(agir)*, a dynamic process of self-producing, and, on the other hand, in matter.

How might one think, at once and in a unified way, about these two aspects of Being, the process of self-producing and the world of matter? Breton sought first to clarify the notion of "world," seeking to distinguish it from the animal environment that is defined by stimulants and responses. It is Being, he proposed, that is the key to the transformation of an environment into a "world," defining Being here as "that by which the stimulant accedes to the dignity of that which is." Breton recognized an inevitable circularity in this way of proceeding: in a certain sense, that which he was attempting to recognize was already presupposed by his questions. Yet the question of how Being "makes a world" would continue to govern his philosophical reflections.

Breton's *Approches phénoménologiques de l'idée d'être*,[12] published in 1959, continues this inquiry into the relation of Being as self-producing and the world of things. In this work he inserts the process by which Being makes a world into the making of the self. The making of a world, he argues, requires the constitution of a space in which to inscribe the work of our hands; it establishes a home or dwelling place for the self *(chez soi)*. The making of this world depends for intelligibility upon the self, whose nature, to the extent it has one, is to have to be what it is. Being is intelligible through the process by which the self, through its responses and denials, realizes itself in a process that Breton terms "the causality of the self by the self." In this understanding, speech implies an ante-predicative, an illuminating light that is rooted in a fundamental act *(agir)*. Being illuminates the world because it is capable of making a world. In this sense, being can be said to "worldify" *(mondifier)*. In numerous essays Breton would continue to investigate the notion of Being, relating it not only to Thomistic notions such as *esse in, esse ad*, and *causa sui*, but later to Neoplatonism, negative theology, and poetics.

Returning to France in 1957, Breton taught at the Institut

---

[12] Breton, *Situation de la philosophie contemporaine*.

Catholique at Lyon and was soon given the chair in metaphysics formerly occupied by Daniel Lallement at the Institut Catholique in Paris. Although he took seriously his responsibilities in the traditional academic program, the decade of the sixties allowed for considerable curricular experimentation and called for greater student involvement in its presentation. On the nomination of Louis Althusser, he was named as Master of Conferences at the prestigious Ecole normale supérieure in Paris, joining an avant-garde philosophical community at a time of turbulence and change.

The Turn Toward Neoplatonism[13]

In Paris, intellectual interests had moved rapidly from Husserl to questions of existence, Being, and non-being and, eventually, to the assimilation of these questions under the rubric of language. As trends rapidly succeeded one another, Breton observed that a number of debates still centered on the Western tendency toward onto-theology, whether under the mode of Heidegger's différence or Derrida's différance.[14] Although Breton appreciated Heidegger's concern with Being and language, he was bemused by the aura of cult that enshrined the reception of Heidegger's work by some theologians. He appreciated Derrida's critique of logocentrism, but, given his sense of the mind's need for unity, was concerned about the outcome of theories of dissonance. He felt a need for a fresh perspective, for taking the step back from accustomed ways of thinking that might allow for "critical distance." Such a space had been opened up for him in the works of French Neoplatonic philosophers and historians, including Jean Trouillard, Henry Duméry, and Joseph Combès. These scholars had participated in a renaissance of Neoplatonic studies initiated by the new availability of E. R. Dodd's translation of Proclus's *Ele-*

---

[13] See Porter, "Stanislas Breton's Use of Neoplatonism to Interpret the Cross in a Postmodern Setting," in which much of this material first appeared.

[14] Stanislas Breton, *Deux mystiques de l'excès: J. J. Surin et Maître Eckhart* (Paris: Cerf, 1985), 5.

mentatio Theologica.[15] From 1959 to 1967 Breton met nearly every Saturday with Trouillard, Duméry, and Combès to read Neoplatonic texts and discuss their contemporary implications.[16] In their view, Neoplatonic thinkers did more than translate Plato. Their works were a creative innovation, radically reinterpreting Plato in light of his *Parmenides.*

The Neoplatonic Mutation

According to Trouillard, the Neoplatonists made their own the well-known Platonic schema that describes reality as a procession from and reversion to the One. The first hypostasis is entirely negative, disengaging the "nothing." The second strives to constitute "the all" by totalizing the affirmations. Yet the totality that it constructs is not the all. It is the third hypostasis, identified with the soul, that posits the affirmations and negations. In moving through the levels of existence, the soul posits itself in all the conditions of its existence.[17] This Neoplatonic schema provided Breton with a means of thinking in terms of a more cosmic unity while including a function of negation. The One, in Plotinus, cannot be identified with the intelligible, that is, with what the human mind finds intelligible. Rather, this nonidentity is the condition for producing the intelligible.

Breton found in Proclus a theory of the soul's emergence through the making of a world, a process that corresponded with his own understanding of the causality of the self by the self. In the Proclean schema, the soul must move through the levels of existence, separating itself from all the evidence of custom and appearance. As it posits affirmations and negations, the soul posits itself in all the conditions of its existence. Negation has a significant function in this process, but Proclus held a positive view of the role of language and the material world in humankind's return to the One. He believed that the One is

---

[15] Proclus, *Elementatio Theologica,* translated by E.R. Dodds (Oxford: Oxford University Press, 1933).

[16] See Wayne Hankey, "Aquinas' First Principle: Being or Unity," *Dionysius* 4 (1980): 133–72 for a comprehensive analysis of these developments.

[17] Stanislas Breton, *Rien ou quelque chose* (Paris: Flammarion, 1987), 83.

present to all beings, even the lowest orders, because all derives from the One. In his understanding, the soul has radically fallen from the One, and no vestige of it remains in the One. This means that the path to the One must be construed as the self moves within the world of being and language. Instead of turning nostalgically toward a spiritual origin, the soul forges its return only within and through the levels of existence. Rather than purifying the soul of the sensible, the soul purifies the sensible. Thus Proclus recognized a role for theurgy or religious ritual that encompasses all dimensions of reality from the highest to the lowest.[18] The soul, in this understanding, makes its way to the One, not by withdrawal from the world but through responsible engagement within it. Yet the source of this possibility, as described by the Neoplatonists, is a "seed of non-being" with which the self communes in the depths of the soul. When writing on philosophical subjects, Breton freely incorporates Neoplatonic schemas and terminology. In his more specifically religious works, he takes care to distinguish between Christianity and any philosophy, alluding to Neoplatonic terms and schemas in a metaphoric rather than foundational way.

Although many intellectuals in Paris disdained philosophic consideration of religious subjects, Breton found others willing to engage them. Colleagues such as Ricoeur, Levinas, and Derrida were interested in discussing religious texts, both in informal conversation and in debates and colloquies such as those convoked by Castelli in Rome. These debates had begun with discussion of Bultmann's program of demythologization, but soon expanded to include such diverse topics as religious language, Heidegger, hermeneutics, and tradition. Breton sought a way to envisage the relation of metaphysics, theology, and theories of dissonance. Instead of approaching this task through an examination of cultural phenomena, he chose to inquire into the different ways in which these varying tendencies articulate metaphysical space, attempting a rigorous meditation on the condition of their possibility.

---

[18] Hankey, 133–72.

The Principle

The term "principle" served as a key to this kind of reflection. In *Du Principe*,[19] published in 1971, Breton presented a rigorous meditation on the notion of the thinkable. In a world distrustful of absolutes, the metaphysical tendency of such a project, and the very notion of a principle, held its pitfalls. Yet despite the problems surrounding the metaphysics of presence and its related ontologies, Breton remained convinced that the mind's disposition toward a certain unity required expression, accompanied always by rigorous critique. One had to go through metaphysics and ontology, he thought, to go beyond them. The term "principle," which had been used by the Neoplatonists and Thomas Aquinas, evaded some of the risks inherent in the notion of causality. Breton defines the principle as that "from which anything proceeds," underscoring the preposition "from," which suggests at once the dynamism of created being and its dependency on something other than itself. Yet the relationship to the source and origin of Being does not imply similitude, as does the notion of "cause," which seems to claim too much knowledge about the origin of Being by supposing that the cause is reflected in its effects. The principle is the source of the possibility of the making of the self. It is not, however, identical with any created form or reflected in what comes from it.

Because the Principle is "nothing of that which is," Breton sometimes refers to it as "no-thing." In a rigorous meditation on its activity, he uses prepositions to lay hold of a displacement through which free Being is realized. "That by which something is is nothing of that which is." The axiom describes a pure activity that produces the objects of consciousness, but because negation is inherent in the process, it is better described as "méontological." The term principle expresses not a hidden presence that might be recovered but the "emptiness of a distance always to be taken because it is never assured." It de-

---

[19] Stanislas Breton, *Du Principe. Essai sur l'organization du pensable* (Paris: Coed. Aubier, Cerf, Desclée, Delachaux et Niestlé, Desclée de Brouwer, 1971).

mands negation and interrogation of what seems solid and real and of our own fascination with the all.

In describing the operations of the principle in terms of a principle of eminence, of the all, and of negation, Breton sought to define and reconcile different forms of expression. From this understanding came an original insight into negative theology as ultimately positive. Negation serves to assure that the self's genesis proceeds through regulated stages. It does not simply deny Being in the ineffable in order to restore it to greater glory. Rather, it is the generative power of the nothing that makes possible the spirit's self-constitution and autonomy, the birth of self and world. At the same time, within the domain of speech, negative theology corrects the tendency to say too much. The principle, because it is nothing of that which proceeds from it, transcends all philosophical or religious determinations. Thus, though human beings must make use of words to reach out to the ineffable, their language requires a negative theology that recognizes the "as if" quality of all affirmations. Breton proposes that the divine names do not lay hold of that which is beyond Being. Rather, they express the presence in the heart of the spirit of an emptiness whose gift is to give what it is not and has not. The negations with which we affect it are converted under its encouraging flux into affirmations and positions that constitute the free becoming of spiritual beings and the consistency of a universe. For Breton, what is commonly called ontology is but the discursive trace of a more profound ontogenesis, expressing the méontological energy of the "nothing."[20]

Etre, Monde, Imaginaire

To further clarify the relation between being and language, Breton's *Etre, Monde et Imaginaire*[21] presents the unfolding of Being in language as the play of logos and mythos. Breton begins his inquiry, as Paul Ricoeur has observed, at the place from which humans work and speak and thus "mean" (*veut-dire*).[22]

---

[20] See Stanislas Breton, "Examen particulier," in Giard, ed., 7–13.

[21] Breton, *Etre, Monde et Imaginaire*.

[22] Ricoeur, "Logos, Mythos, Stauros," 126.

Yet this space or orientation in which language and action are inscribed implies a pre-predicative. Signification is articulated in a determined space, but implies a condition of possibility that exceeds it. Breton calls this condition of possibility that both limits discourse and makes it possible the "imaginary nothing" *(rien imaginaire)*. It is accessible to us only through reflection upon the will, requiring first a theory of logos, and second, a space of the word for myth and fable. Desire *(vouloir)* is characterized both by a tendency toward Being as logos and a tendency toward the involuntary *(non-vouloir)* that tends toward myth. As Jean Greisch notes,[23] Breton describes the discourse of Being as articulated in the double register of ontology and onto-mythology, both of which are needed for a comprehension of Being.

The "nothing" that gives rise to speech is not inert but active. As Breton relates the "nothing" to the imaginary, to the Word and its fulgurations, to play, he insists above all on its power. This power comprises at once the attraction of Being toward the nothing and the procession of nothing toward Being. It elicits both the *causa sui* and, in turn, the thought of death; it is both generative and reductive. Thus a paradoxical axiom governs the possibility of language and its limits: "That by which something comes to be is nothing of that which is." In terms of religious language, it is because there is an ineffable that we are bound to speak. Yet, although the "imaginary nothing" gives rise to the word, it is not the Word. It has the power to make speech possible, but also to displace that speech toward service and action.

Political and Religious Writings

Breton's interest in theory was always closely related to political and spiritual praxis; he has always insisted that philosophy must be rooted in the life of the world. Teaching at a period of persuasive Marxist intellectual influence, he frequently discussed

---

[23] Jean Greisch, "L'ontologie, l'ontomythologie et l'imaginaire-Rien," in Giard, ed., 23–24.

xviii   TRANSLATOR'S INTRODUCTION

Marxist thought with his friend Louis Althusser and with the many workers in his circle of family and friends. Although he vocally opposed Stalinism and resisted the identification of Christianity with any party, he saw Marxism as a catalyst to Christian thought, reminding it of the Gospel's call to justice and material service. He found kinship with the Marxist emphasis upon critical distance and on the importance of the future. Yet he also believed the seductiveness of such a thought required a theory of ideology. In works such as *Théorie des idéologies* (1976),[24] *Spinoza, théologie et politique* (1977)[25] and *Marxisme et critique* (1979)[26] Breton explores the notion of displacement illustrated in an "operator of transcendence" and offers a theory of ideology.

In *Ecriture et révélation*[27] (1979), Breton turned to a more specifically religious subject, raising the question of writing and revelation in a postmodern framework that looks back to Proclean Neoplatonism. He faces the problem of a plurality of meanings in scripture, and grounds his understanding of its formation through an analogy with a person "writing the self in the world," according to a fundamental Being in the world that is open to an infinite possibility of expressions. Similarly, he sees, in the world, a presence of the Word that is open to various forms of writing and finds its scriptural expression in light of Christ and the Cross. Although Breton situates his task here in relation to Heidegger and Kant, he bases his own retrieval on notions drawn from Proclus on the relation of the one and the many, inclusive of negation.

THE WORD AND THE CROSS

These reflections were furthered in 1981, when Breton published *The Word and the Cross,* a work that crystallized his meditations on the Cross as well as his philosophic questions. The work is continuous with his philosophical project, even though,

[24] Stanislas Breton, *Théorie des idéologies* (Paris: Desclée, 1976).
[25] Stanislas Breton, *Spinoza, théologie et politique* (Paris: Desclée, 1977).
[26] Stanislas Breton, *Marxisme et critique* (Paris: Desclée, 1979).
[27] Stanislas Breton, *Ecriture et Révélation* (Paris, Cerf, 1979)

as Breton himself insists, the Cross is not a philosophical theorem. As Paul Ricoeur has observed, *The Word and the Cross*
"begins with a word that precedes it."[28] By contrasting Pauline
and Johannine texts, Breton asks here how the Word comes
forth in the world and assumes some form of human expression,
some form of human speech. The excursus first examines the
way in which the power of the Word finds expression under
Paul's threefold designation of logos, folly, and power. It then
examines the way in which kenosis transforms religious language and its determinations, contrasting this language of
kenosis to the splendid fulgurations of the Johannine Word.
Breton then considers the Cross today and some of the questions it addresses to contemporary faith.

According to well-known critiques of logocentrism, Christianity had been influenced, from its origins, by a dual Greek
and Jewish heritage. Its thought, guided by key terms of its vocabulary, inclined it to seek a unifying divine purpose behind its
scriptures rather than allowing for the diversity encouraged by
the Jewish tradition of commentary. This "onto-theological" and
"logocentric" tendency has contributed to a kind of violence by
which Christianity welcomes sameness and represses difference. *The Word and the Cross* makes no specific reference to
this critique. Yet Breton roots his reflection in texts that speak
specifically of Christian origins, of Logos, of Greek and Jew, and
of Being. Taking up a language vulnerable to critique, he re-
thinks texts and terms in a way opened up by the presence, at
the heart of these texts, of a Sign of contradiction. The Cross
exercises a méontological function upon all religious language.
In its reductive and generative power, it continues to promise,
despite the dangers inherent in its destiny in the world, the
possibility of something new.

The Cross in the World of Language[29]

The work takes as its starting point Paul's first letter to the Corinthians (1 Cor. 1–17), analyzing the language through which

[28] Ricoeur, "Logos, Mythos, Stauros," 125.
[29] See Porter, "Stanislas Breton's Use of Neoplatonism to Interpret the
Cross in a Postmodern Setting," in which this discussion first appeared.

Paul describes a community torn by division. The Word has come into the world, and yet the Corinthians cannot arrive at the Name to be proclaimed. The people seek a common spirit and sense of belonging, through pledges of allegiance that imply the superiority of the cause to which they commit themselves. Each invokes a name, "I, I am of Apollo," "I, I am of Paul," "I, I am of Christ." Breton points to the paradoxical structure of this language, noting that the accent on the name proclaimed shifts toward the "I" that proclaims it. The name to be exalted seems to disappear in the proprietary speech of the one who exalts it (10–11). Breton pinpoints in these claims a universal mechanism of the ego that easily becomes embedded in religious language. Faced with what it lacks in itself, the ego tries to recover itself by exalting the excellence of that which it desires.

Breton relates the problem at Corinth to a fundamental problem of religious language that occurs as people reach out from their dividedness toward one who might unite them. The situation evokes Neoplatonism, sketching the movement of the multiple toward the One and need for negation it implies. In Corinth, the desire to be is concretized in all its vulnerability to distortion. The problem that Paul identifies is not in the order of knowledge, for even those who claim allegiance to Christ misuse the Name. They seek to lay hold of what cannot be encompassed in any form of language, discipleship, or institution. The issue here is not which leader is to be named, for as Breton observes, "Even the name of Christ seems to be no more than the flag held high by a sect of followers" (**present volume, 10**). The problem here is that the ego seeks to found itself, making its own instinctual need the measure of reality. Its rhetorical superlatives betray a possessive desire for riches, so that even the religious impulse tends toward the false attribution.

Breton recognizes in these religious assertions a universal desire for unity that finds expression in religious language. And yet the claims fall short of the mark. The Corinthians seek unity and belonging, and yet they do not perceive that the totality they construct is not the all. The problem within the situation at Corinth is that those who claim to belong to some special group cannot stop midway. In such partisan speech, Breton

notes, "The atom is made to stand out, making itself the constitutive force, the unique element of the whole ensemble"(11).
Thus, although people reach out for unity and belonging, they
assert a partisanship that can only end in schism. The problem
at Corinth, for Breton, illustrates at Christianity's beginnings
the pitfalls of religious language and action that require a principle of critique and redirection.

How, then, does Paul move the community from schism to
unity, from egotistic self-preoccupation to the works of the new
creation? Breton stresses the bold question with which Paul
stops contention in its tracks. He silences the babble of divided
tongues with a simple interrogation: "Is it then Paul who has
been crucified for you?" The sign of the Cross, in which the
very appearing of the Word has been negated, opens a hiatus.
Breton suggests here that absolute truth does not lie in anything
external, in a person, a message or an institution. The Cross is a
reminder that there is no direct road to knowledge of the deity,
that the ego is not God. To think this is to inflate the ego. The
Cross, by its negation, makes it clear that even the coherence of
the community must be subordinated to the authenticity of this
message. The Sign of contradiction silences competing claims,
injecting a question mark into the discourse of desire. In this
quiet space, the Cross points toward a "beyond" *(au delà)* that
cannot be encompassed within the structures of thought and
language. It opens up a path to be followed.

The *Logos Staurou*

This sign of contradiction, in its power of negation, interrogates
the very world of language from which the Corinthians draw
their speech and thought. It calls logos itself into question. The
Pauline text, he observes, speaks of *Logos staurou*, a Logos of
the Cross **(9–10)**. Although many translators simply transcribe
logos as word or message, Breton asks the reader to ponder the
phrasing of the Greek text. Too facile a translation suppresses
the jarring dissimilarity of the words that Paul has joined together. It misses the fine point of the text, Breton insists, which
lies precisely in the startling juxtaposition of the two antithetical

Greek words, *logos* and *staurou*. Although Paul is concerned with intelligibility, the enigmatic phrase yields no apparent message. The notion of a *logos staurou* is a contradiction in terms, setting against the notion of logos the paradoxical figure of the "suffering servant" who is obedient to death, even to the death of the Cross (**9**). Thus this text on Christian beginnings recalls a sign of contradiction at the heart of Christian language. It is not a word among other words but stops their flow. This sign of contradiction, this *logos staurou*, provides faith with a principle of critique and innovation that has the possibility of transforming religious language.

In his attention to the function of negation in this passage, Breton evokes the role of negative theology. The Cross that Paul holds up interrupts rhetorical excess, as the negative theologies of a later day would interrogate the language of the divine names. Before the Word can be preached, Paul must recall for the Corinthians the Cross that negates speech. At the same time, that Cross recalls the death of Christ in which the very appearing of the Word was negated. In words reminiscent of Proclus, Breton notes that it is "as if there were an ever concealed affinity between the nothing and the One" (**12**). The Cross recalls the self-emptying of the divine, even as it interrogates the human ego. From a union with Christ in the depths of the soul, the believer learns the language of self-emptying and service. To speak of this ascesis, Breton uses imagery drawn from the Neoplatonists, who privileged the "null point" of emptiness in which the soul finds union with the One as it follows the path it has traced.

Athens and Jerusalem

Although Breton refers to Neoplatonic schemas of cosmic dimensions, he situates his analysis of the text in the concrete world in which Christianity took root. In that culture, Christians were destined to speak the language of Jew and Greek. Paul must maintain a foothold in that world of language if he is to speak convincingly at all. Breton insists here that Athens and Jerusalem do not represent alternatives, one of which can be chosen over the other. Rather, they epitomize a dual heritage that can never entirely be set aside. Paradoxically, when preached within these conditions of language and culture, the Cross urges faith to move beyond their limits.

In Breton's view, Paul makes a heuristic use of this typology, setting before the Corinthians the two prevailing modes of religious response within their culture. The notion of the "Greek," for example, illustrates a way of conceiving of God as sovereign intelligence, while that of the "Jew" represents a notion of God as sovereign will. The "Greek" type calls to mind the search for wisdom informed by reason and inquiring into the internal and external causes of the world. That of the "Jew" evokes a desire for acts that people can admire. Seeking a sovereign will behind these acts, it asks "Who has done this?" or "Why has such an adversity occurred?" Paul neither makes a judgment on other religions nor demands that the faithful choose one over the other. His intent is simply to represent the prevailing religious culture. Decisively, he demands a rupture with that culture, insisting that "While the Jews demand miracles and the Greeks look for wisdom, we are preaching a crucified Christ." Christians, though they must speak in the language of Greek and Jew, must move beyond these constructs. The new wine cannot be poured into old wineskins (**14–17**).

Later generations will attempt to dissolve the tension between Athens and Jerusalem in a false synthesis that some thinkers will call "onto-theological." The Word can never entirely escape that destiny, for it must find expression in some form of human speech. Yet the Cross demands that religious language be used with a sense of the need for continual dispossession. As Breton has observed elsewhere, "we are inevitably committed to this philosophical exodus, this vacillation between two homes of thought. We have left the home of Israel just as we have left the home of Greece. We remain homesick for both."[30] The Corinthians must submit themselves to the unnamable One, to the ineffable Word whose very coming forth is negated on the Cross. They cannot entirely escape their linguis-

---

[30] Kearney, *States of Mind: Dialogues with Contemporary Thinkers*, 250.

tic destiny, but they can submit their words and works to the judgment of the Cross.

A New Way of Being

Reversing prevailing cultural values, Paul presents the power of the Cross as logos, folly, and power. This threefold designation guides Breton in his examination of the way in which the Word of the Cross has come into the world. He first examines logos by contrasting the theologies of Aquinas and Bultmann, especially in their understanding of Being, clarifying the limits of theology before the judgment of the Cross. As logos intersects mythos, he then turns toward the margins of Christian life and worship through a more poetic reminiscence of the "fools of Christ." Although he recognizes the power of the Cross, he also must demonstrate irony of its destiny before the "powers" in history. The Cross retains its power, but it is the power of the "nothing." As Paul Ricoeur has noted, if there is a driving force in Breton's thought, it is indeed the power of the nothing: "To annihilate being, logos, myth, world—that is power."[31] The Cross is nothing that people in their reason, desire, or history want it to be. And yet, it is by being nothing of that which is that the Word has the possibility to become all things.

Kenosis and Metaphor

To further clarify this function of the Cross, Breton juxtaposes his exegesis of the First Epistle to the Corinthians with an interpretation of Paul's hymn in the Epistle to the Philippians (2, 5–11). He observes, first, that the notion of kenosis has always eluded adequate theological interpretation. Paul speaks of the indwelling in God of Jesus Christ, "who, though he was in the form of God, did not consider equality with God as a thing to be grasped" (Phil.2:1). The text characterizes relations within the Godhead in terms of both indwelling and a need for dispossession, concepts that recall for Breton the Thomistic notions of

---

[31] Ricoeur, "Logos, Mythos, Stauros," 125.

"being in" *(esse in)* and "being toward" *(esse ad)*. In Paul, a tendency toward dispossession appears as a movement *ad extra* that is not a simple manifestation or epiphany. Rather, it is a descent and ascent through a series of stages: subsistence in God, the assumption of a human form, the obedience of the servant unto the death on the Cross, ascent and Glory **(133– 135)**. Moreover, the death of Christ is not simply a negation of negative death. In his death, something happens that can never be effaced, and this cannot simply be described as the negation of a negation. It is a movement that goes beyond death's negation into God, through the negation. As resurrection overcomes death, it achieves its counterpoint. The Resurrected one emerges from the non-being of death. The schema suggests that through taking the form of the suffering servant, something occurs in this divine "suffering servant" that resembles a becoming. At the same time the created world assumes a new relation to the divine.

Various attempts have been made to explain this mystery in a way that preserves transcendence while doing justice to the implicit movement *ad extra*. To demonstrate the difficulties inherent in these projects, Breton points out interpretations that emphasize either the divine immutability or the suffering of God, contrasting them with an interpretation of the Sufi understanding of the divine compassion **(135–148)**. None of these, in Breton's view, does full justice to the problematic. He prefers to focus upon the way in which Paul's language effects a change in his listeners. Rather than deriving from the hymn a concept of God, he considers the way in which the power of the Word transforms language.

This transformation affects the very vocabulary familiar within Paul's social milieu. Paul taps into the imagery of master and servant to describe metaphorically the divine kenosis, tracing a passage toward servanthood, from ineffability through the form of *doulos* or slave, a figure so familiar yet despised within that hierarchical organized setting **(149–150)**. It is this use of metaphor that dismantles a world of habitual expectations. As the figure of the *doulos* is assumed, a certain image of the divine dies, and with it die settled distinctions between master and

servant, rich and poor, dominator and oppressed. A new and
kenotic image of the divine appears, in the image of "the suffering servant" who became obedient unto death.

The Cross thus becomes the a priori of human perception,
shaping thought of divine and human. Through this displacement of language the image of the suffering servant invites a
corresponding practice of faith, illustrated in Matthew 25,
35–46: "I was hungry; I was thirsty; I was naked; I was a
stranger." "Each time you did it to one of these little ones you
did it to me." Its judgment esteems nothing that common religious sense would expect: cult, adoration, submission to transcendent Truth. The face of God emerges in those "who are
not." The judgment of the Cross privileges the language of service, which reaches, out of nothingness, to others. Thus the
Cross does not relegate the divine to ineffability. Rather, in this
last judgment, through kenosis a mysterious and divine "I" appears, imploring for the disinherited with whom he had identified himself, the future of a "human being," that he has not and
that he is not but which will give him the just response of a
creative generosity.

Philosophy and Exegesis

In response to the largely sympathetic reading of *The Word and
the Cross* by Paul Ricoeur, Breton has noted several lacunae in
the work, observing especially the effects of a certain abstract-
ness. He recognizes especially a need to relate the Cross to the
events commemorated by the kerygma and recalled by the
Credo (Passion, death, Resurrection). He admits that his analysis needs to be more consistently related to factuality, and to
appear as it really is: not the explication of a theorem, but the
permanent meaning of a history, in its divine and human destiny.[32] The relation of the *theologia crucis* to issues of election
and unicity might be further pursued. Yet he hopes he has
pointed toward the reality and power of the Cross, made more
apparent by allusions to the "seed of non-being" of Neoplaton-

[32] See Breton, "Examen Particulier," 13–14.

ism and the philosopher's "imaginary nothing" *(imaginaire rien)*. *The Word and the Cross* is a work written from the perspective of faith. The Cross negates all forms of language, returning them to their submission to the Unnamable One, the Word who dwells with the Father and whose very coming forth is negated on the Cross.

Breton's more recent works, *Rien ou quelque chose*[33] (1987) *Poétique du sensible*[34] (1988), *Philosophie buissonnière*[35] (1989), have dwelt upon language and poetics. As Jean Greisch has noted, "It is not by chance that the author of *The Word and the Cross* has chosen to concern himself with these neglected domains of language."[36]

Because of Breton's intrepidity in face of issues, his work is not without problems. It will invite critique from different sides. Especially when writing on religious subjects, Breton insists that his words not be taken as theological statements, for they flow out of a philosopher's vocation to provoke thought. *The Word and the Cross,* like its author, defies any easy classification or any facile explication. This introduction and translation intends simply to provide readers with an opportunity to view the range of possibility that this original and creative work affords.

---

[33] Breton, *Rien ou quelque chose.*

[34] Stanislas Breton, *Poétique du sensible* (Paris: Cerf, 1988).

[35] Stanislas Breton, *Philosophie buissonnière* (Grenoble: Jérôme Millon, 1989).

[36] Greisch, 22.

The Word and the Cross

1

A Word of Folly

THIS DISCOURSE on the Word will pass between two Pauline texts, which serve as two columns of fire that fix the boundaries of speech. The first reflects Paul's preaching (1 Cor. 1,17–31); the other resonates, even its ordered measure, to the fervor of a hymn (Phil. 2, 5–11). I will begin by listening to the first text, holding in balance its relationship to the second, and then proceed more directly to the hymn to further clarify its sense. The relationship can be set from the start, in what may seem an abrupt shortcut, by saying that the Word of the Cross effectuates the transcendence of the *Logos* by setting it over against the paradoxical figure of the servant who is obedient to death, even to death on the Cross. The Cross is thus the place where two excesses intersect, the one by which thought itself is outpassed, the other where willing ceases, especially the willing of oneself in any form.

I. *LOGOS* AND *STAUROS*

There is something unusual about the relation of the two Greek terms *Logos* and *Stauros*. The Pauline expression *Logos Staurou*, the Logos of the Cross, which unites them, could also be reversed. Could it not be said that it is precisely the Logos that is crossed, that it is the Cross of the Logos that is evoked? This is indeed, it seems, the fine point of Paul's exhortation. To establish this viewpoint, we must start with some preliminaries.

1. The function of the Cross, and of the Word that makes it known, becomes clear against the background of the division run rampant that it would remedy. Effectively, schisms and quarrels divide the community of Corinth. Each faction invokes a name (Paul, Apollo, or Cephas) that becomes for it a slogan

and point of honor. Even the name of Christ seems to be no more than a flag held high by a sect of followers. Would the principle of unity be thus divided, and divided against itself? Is it not necessary, transcending partisan claims, to bring everything back in unity to the same, to the same force that gives rise to the one and necessary Word *(Parole)* that harmonizes the indeed necessary differences, uniting them in a common spirit *(nous)* and in common purpose *(gnome)*? That which gathers is presented here under the figures of Word and Spirit, which give rise to a certain fundamental way of feeling and a state of consciousness that is the common experience of all. This Same should scatter those forces of dispersion that set sects alongside one another, each in its egocentric way claiming the mantle of a prestigious and controlling name: I, I am of Paul, or I, I am of Christ, etc. By a strange inversion of relations, the one to whom ownership is ceded by a grammatical twist in the use of the genitive, in fact disappears in face of the proprietary claims of the one who stakes out the proper use of this name. When one yields to the temptation of schism, even when this means adhering to some special group, it is impossible to stop midway. The atom is as it were made to stand out, so that it is the constitutive force, the unique element of the whole ensemble. The logician speaks in this respect of the singleton, the one that belongs in a series but stands out alone in it, as does a card in a pack. Popular language sums it up by use of the word "singular."

Yet the abuse made of it does not discredit a proper use of the term "to be of," which figures in the proposition: I, I am of Paul, or of Apollo. The mistake made by the Apollonians was to confiscate the form of Christ from any further use than theirs, as though like a sponge it could be saturated and filled up by pouring into it all that is peculiar to themselves. The Apostle clearly sees this to be impossible, though it is well understood that he too belongs to Christ, that he too is "of Christ." This relational language, which we will continue to use in what follows, is as characteristic of the New as it is of the Old Testament. In the Pauline epistles, the prepositions *in, by,* and *with,* when used with the name of Christ, are what most often indicate Christian life. This is so much the case that the being of the Christian could well be defined by a transitive relation, or more precisely by a description of relation, whether individual or plural. Even in the latter case, in which the relation is ascribed to a plurality, one does well to remember that in the New Testament there is a tendency to take as a concrete whole, as an individual being, the ensemble or whole class of subjects who refer themselves to Christ. One speaks of the Church of Christ, or of the Body of Christ, as of a single individual with a given relation to Christ, himself unique and singular. This observation holds true also when it is a question of the Cross, of Christ Crucified, of those who are of him or not of him. The ensemble of persons who are united or made one by the Sign of contradiction has nothing to do with a logical or social abstraction, with a category of persons. It is a living whole that Paul perceives, seen in its relation to the one in whom it has being and movement. In this respect, the use of the expressions "to be of" or "to be in" only vaguely refers to some simple act of belonging to a logical unit. These expressions are more appropriately to be taken in the strongest sense of oneness, connoting a milieu in which those who belong of and in are bathed, or a unique cause to which they are unconditionally devoted and by reason of which they have their very existence.

2. It is precisely the contrast between the illusory schismatic of belonging to a quarrelsome group, and a true belonging to the spirit and way of Christ, that provokes the dazzling interrogation: "Is it then Paul who was crucified for you?" "Is it in his name that you were baptized?" The Cross, whose message he carries, emerges suddenly to cast light upon the misery of the divisions that nourish themselves endlessly on their excessive rhetoric. It is the Cross that unites those whom an apparent wisdom divides, as if there were an ever-concealed affinity between the Nothing and the One.

Perhaps, after all, for this Unity to appear, divisions must have made its necessity all too clear. Thus the relation of division to oneness is comparable to that of the specter of contradiction that in the universe of logic serves as a background to the declaration of the principle of noncontradiction.

A unified church is not, however, the sole concern motivating

Paul's address to the Corinthians. The Apostle's mission, that for which he was sent, is precisely to proclaim the Cross, the Cross that stands firm even through and over against all this division. It is this power that even our insignificant praises always risk rendering vain.

"The Logos of the Cross, for those who are lost is folly, but for those who are saved, for us, it is the power of God" (v. 18). I will for the moment avoid any translation of this term, *Logos*, for it is here invoked in a way that is alien to its more or less classic significance. The biblical equivalent that is often proposed would be adequate only if it were shown that when forced to choose between the alternatives of Greek and Jew, Paul could liberate himself from the first only by abandoning himself to the second. Such is, however, not the case, for the entire thought process that unfolds in the following verses shows clearly the effort to speak the unheard by transcending the disjunction between Greek and Jew. "Christ crucified, folly for the Gentiles, is also scandal for the Jews." It is, therefore, to be expected that no translation of *Logos,* whatever it might be, would be equal to the force of the original affirmation. "The Greeks seek wisdom, the Jews demand signs. As for us, we proclaim Christ crucified." The rupture is sharp. Even if Paul judges that what he preaches has meaning for the one as for the other, in the measure to which all are called, it does not follow that an amalgam emerges from the process in which divisions are wiped out. It is not necessary to overcome the division of the religious humanity of his time into two parts, unequal, to be sure, in their numerical strength, by using the cover of a synthesis that reconciles opposites. The aim of the Pauline text is evidently to suggest something else to us, through the help of a simple typology that characterizes in broad strokes the fundamental attitudes that fall under the designation of the respective names, "the Jews" and "the Greeks."

II. The Fundamental Attitudes

1. We should not expect from Paul a history of Greek philosophy. The word *Greek* for him does not just name the people of

a geographic region but sums up a certain way of perceiving God, humanity, the world. In a rudimentary religious phenomenology that accents the religious, the "Greek" (in its neutral meaning of power and élan: *to hellenikon*) represents an attitude that can be specified by the verb "to search." He is concerned with the "Greeks" as he would be with the sect of Sceptics, if he knew them. They serve here as an illustration or paradigm. Paul wants to typify the kind of searching linked to the exigencies of this people's temperament, as expressed in the Platonic construction *logon didonai*, "to realize, to give reasons." Under the sign of the principle of reason, the "Greek" represents reason immanent in things themselves, or a reason that is exterior to them. In turn, the exigency of reason under these two modalities motivates the questions organized most often under the genres of causality: those that explain the world in its structure and becoming and those that explain its meaning and finality.

This Greek universe, dominated by the "idea," can thus be named *Cosmos*—with all this term connotes of beauty, light, and harmony—without losing sight of the Good that our ontological tradition, diluting the force of the original, joins to the classic transcendentals of being, the one and the true. Paul has no doubt that this world is eminently religious. If the discourse attributed to him on the hill of Ares is really his, the "Greeks" for him were "the most religious of people."

2. The Jews were not seekers of this kind. At the risk of oversimplification, we would say that their fundamental attitude comes to expression in the verb *claim*, as opposed to *seek*. What do they claim? Not reasons for which one searches but *signs*, marvels that manifest an admirable and incomprehensible power that irrupts, in a sudden burst, to upset our calculations and disconcert our wisdom. These signs—that is to say, wonders—solicit less a question than the appreciation of an Excellence who can generously dispense exception. What moves this fundamental attitude is not a principle of reason but a principle of arbitrary sovereignty that one would not know how to interrogate because it undercuts the ground for inquiring into its inner being and activity. It requires a more personal starting point.

Who did this? And above all, why this adversity or failure when
one considered oneself sheltered within the collective self-
consciousness by a privilege of uniqueness and exception?

From these observations, if we have not moved too far from
the text, we can offer a schema of an elementary phenomenology of religious consciousness, in its two forms par excellence:

Religious Consciousness

A. In its Greek form　1. Attitude: wisdom and quest
　　　　　　　　　　　2. Motor of the attitude: principle of
　　　　　　　　　　　　 reason
　　　　　　　　　　　3. Kinds of questions: internal and
　　　　　　　　　　　　 external causes of the world

B. In its Jewish form　1. Attitude: demand for signs,
　　　　　　　　　　　　 admiration
　　　　　　　　　　　2. Motor of the attitude: principle of
　　　　　　　　　　　　 arbitrary sovereignty
　　　　　　　　　　　3. Kinds of questions: Who did this?
　　　　　　　　　　　　 Why this adversity?

III. A Certain *Beyond*

1. It is against this pre-understanding or global horizon that we
must understand the decisive rupture Paul brings to the fore in
this text. If the Cross is folly for the Gentiles, it is also scandal
for the Jews. Consequently, "the Logos, that of the Cross" can
be interpreted under neither the Greek nor the Old Testament
rubric. Yet for the people of that time, these were the sole alternatives. Since Paul rejects them, the negation of the disjunction
is equivalent here, as in good logic, to the conjunction of two
negations. The double repudiation, seeming surprisingly proud,
is reinforced by the repetition of the article "*the* Logos, that of
the Cross," giving it the value not only of the specific indicative
but of unicity. The singular condition of this Logos drains or
consumes the ensemble to which it belongs. As a result it eludes
classification under any common genre in which it would stand

side by side with something else. More precisely, since it is a question here of two opposites, the reiteration of the article marks the impossibility of pouring the new wine into languages that cannot be vessels for it.

2. Yet after we have waived aside as "inessential" distinctions that disturbed the first community and divided Western humanity along religious lines, a new partition of another nature emerges. The alternative now confronts two classes of people: "the saved" and "the lost." This *decisive* opposition (in the etymological sense of the term) reactivates the radicality of the former in the language of being or non-being. But "being" and "non-being" here do not arise out of a formal ontology. Rather, they signify "salvation" and "perdition," terms that evoke more than the ancient distinction between possession and privation. Beneath the Cross, the parting of the waters does more than divide two groups. It invites them to declare themselves "for" or "against" the Cross. Such is the judgment on the world. But in pronouncing a judgment on the Cross, one judges oneself and thus makes oneself what one is. Those who see in the Sign of contradiction only misery and insignificance find folly and infirmity. The wisdom and power they give themselves determine the limits of their prison and the true extent of their fall. To those who overcome the appearances of the world, this "Nothing" motions from the shadows. It points beyond wisdom and power, making them wiser and stronger by being nothing of that which it gives. The text, with what appears as sectarian self-satisfaction, does speak of folly being on the side of wisdom and wisdom on the side of folly. Yet this reversal is just good rhetoric. It is not surprising that having so sharply evoked the chasm, Paul hastens to fill it by restoring to the negative the glory of eminence. Those who preach the new language must draw upon the old or risk sounding schizophrenic. If the Cross is not of this world, it remains no less in this world. And this destiny, which appears in our text in this first collapse of language, will not cease, in the course of centuries, to weigh upon its history.

3. The shameful sign that reverses common sense establishes a principle of judgment that scoffs at evidence. What counts by

common reckoning matters little to the regard that measures it from the height of the Cross. We rediscover here, but on another level, the critique of appearances. It is as if what seems to be self-evident and necessary by custom is only, at the core, a contingency that doesn't know itself as such. In theological language, we express this paradox as a divine predilection "which chooses that which is weak according to the world to confound the strong"(vv. 27–28). Is not the death of evidence, here as well as elsewhere, the true beginning? God has chosen that which is not *(me onta)* to suspend (or put in parentheses) that which is *(ta onta)*.

4. This inversion of prerogatives that affirm "that which is not," the calling into question of the universally accepted, elicits a double set of objections. I will pass over the charge of absurdity because it takes us too far from the text. A law of logic, well-known under the term paradoxical implication, recalls that if a proposition is absurd, false, or impossible it may, strictly and materially, imply nothing at all. The medievals already specified that "from the absurd" nothing whatever follows. If one measures the Pauline text by the logician's ruler, not much remains. Permitting all things, it yields itself to the caprices of chance. The folly of the Cross brings us to chaos. It suggests less the critique of order than the impossibility of realizing it, as quivering atoms that seem free because they are incapable of making something be, but dream of "a state of paradise before the world was made." I willingly agree that Paul is no logician. But this is perhaps because he speaks of "something else" and because this disturbing "other" deserves at least to be presented to our thought.

5. The real difficulty concerns the remainder of the text and the gospel of the beatitudes as well: the exceptional lot set aside for "that which is not." Does not this morbid predilection for non-being merely reflect the impotence of tired souls who invest that which possesses being and value with the sadness of their own failed lives and their anger of destructive resentment?

The question is yet more compelling because the text stresses the humble state of the Christians of Corinth ("There are not many sage, powerful or noble among you" [vv. 26–27]), acknowledging an explicit affinity that links the modesty of their condition with the infirmity of the crucified, as if in the similitude of subject and object of faith, the God of the poor could be nothing but a poor God. In recalling the Cross, does not raising up the wise and powerful in any way not break the bond of homogeneity, sinning by incoherence? But if this is so, is it not precisely because the poor, far from rejecting the values of the world and envisaging a God who shares their poverty, seek spontaneously a God of richness and power who, in order to fill up their want, sublimates in his eminence all known perfections and nobilities? What we will call later "the analogy of the divine names" tried to give learned expression to this axiology of common sense and very popular addition in which the limits of excellence are suppressed only to push them to the supreme degree, that is, to the divine. Thus poverty risks, contrary to what we might expect, exalting into a *summum* those "grandeurs of the flesh" that provisionally elude our striving. The Apostle's warning is aimed precisely at mortifying this natural inclination. It goes directly to the appetite. The God of the Cross is not the God of desire. And that is why this God does now know how to be a God of the superlative, as if the superlative already betrayed within language the first intrusion of divinity. In this respect, as well as being a critique of the divine names, the folly of the Cross is a critique of the first movements of the soul and of a certain "transcendent psychology." And the relation of the condition of the faithful and the God of the Cross implies less the duplication of the finite in the infinite than the emergence of a nude and sublime point at which faith cannot be distinguished from its object because the idolatrous, on either side, has ceased to be the norm of judgment.

6. There is another exegesis that also underscores the epistle's stress on the opposition between "that which is" and "that which is not." But this reading seeks to uncover there, though cast in religious form, the immemorial class struggle of the oppressors and the oppressed. Here an intolerable inequality perceived in the contrast between having and not having, between power and wisdom on the one hand and the social condition of the poor, incites the just resentment of the exploited, who in

the name of justice demand an end to this state of violence. It is true that religion, even while condemning the order of excellence that language consecrates, risks blunting the edge of an unvoiced rebellion by transmuting its energy into a transcendent problematic, and the Pauline text cannot elude this danger. Yet despite this real pitfall, the text offers within the Western tradition the first protest given by the Word on behalf of those who do not exist and have the right to exist. In this respect, we cannot underestimate the magnitude of a protest that calls into question the ancient God of wisdom and of power, keeper and guardian of the established world. From now on, this God is dead "in Jesus Christ," whose Cross, elevated above the powers to signify the end of their too long reign, upholds the struggle of an "empty" class, raising consciousness of its dignity and strength. Of course, this proud interpretation emerges from a sociopolitical milieu that it reflects in its own way. Yet it is more and better than a lifeless and faithful image of it. It marks the beginning of a transformative movement that will resurge in its time in the scientific and political theory of a party that, by right at least, is universal.

The second interpretation, often linked to the defense of the poor in the prophetic tradition and with the hard sayings of the Gospel on riches and power, is not exorbitant in itself. It emerges from a context of authenticity in which the memorable words "that which you have done to the least among you, you do unto me" confirms that the scope of justice must be wide as the world. Its fault is not that it reminds us of what we have forgotten or left to the initiatives of private charity, but that it has lacked lucidity about its own positions. I will examine later the different hypotheses that enable us to see this more clearly. In anticipation, it is important to recall the breadth of this horizon, despite the dangers of anthropocentrism. If the folly of the Cross has a meaning that is more than our desire, it probably cannot be reduced in the way we would like it to be.

7. These critical observations have but one end: to bring us to the focal point of the text, where we find manifest a meaning and semantic energy of which the Apostle himself is but the echo and place of passage. The Cross is presented effectively as

Logos, Folly *(Moria)*, and Power *(Dunamis)*. Theoretically, these three elements yield six permutations. The play of possibilities does not concern us directly. Yet it permits us to glimpse displacements of accent that are not without importance, whether from the perspective of logic or history. Here lies the legitimacy of a twofold question: How, over the course of the centuries, have these three elements been valorized? What is, or what might be now, the logical order of these factors? We will examine first the modes of presentation or diverse inflections that have specified Christian consciousness of the Cross in its Western development.

2

The Theologies of the Cross

I AM WRITING neither a history of devotion to the cross nor a psychology of the attitudes of the epochs that have left their imprint upon the Sign of contradiction. More modestly, by following the main themes of the Pauline text, I intend to inquire into the most striking forms or tendencies that may be taken by the three "staurological" elements: Logos, folly, and power. In fact, at the mercy of affinities or vocations, one or another of these elements emerges in such relief that an equally important "moment" recedes to the background. Thus history divides with a necessary bias what the initial structure, in its internal logic, forbids us to separate. We perceive then a multiplicity of perspectives or experiences, each within its limits honoring the mystery it strives to recover. If I did not fear falling under the shadow of a great masterpiece, I would risk the adaptation of a "phenomenology of the spirit" to the Cross.

To avoid the difficulty of beginnings, I will follow the Epistle's own order (loosely enough to modify it later). I will therefore examine first the historical projection of the Logos of the Cross in the discourse of theology.

The term "theology of the Cross" recalls the Lutheran *theologia crucis*, itself opposed to a *theologia gloriae*, too human, perhaps, because enslaved to its profane foundations. I will enlarge this field of reference, however, in order to encompass here two very different kinds of "staurological discourse," illustrating these exemplary forms through the respective concepts of Thomas Aquinas and R. Bultmann.

I. THE THOMISTIC EXEGESIS

Aquinas presents his understanding in his commentary on the First Epistle to the Corinthians. I will condense its essence here.

1. When Paul impugns the "wisdom of the Word," there is no doubt he excludes recourse to a strident rhetoric that would be incompatible with sober preaching and respect for the listener. Yet the interdiction concerns more than a way of speaking. It bears also and above all "on the wisdom of the word, that is to say on human reason, because the things of faith surpass rational proceedings." Does it follow, then, that reason must be rejected in the name of the Cross? That interpretation would go beyond the letter and intention of the text. The difficulty can be resolved if an important distinction is kept in mind. After all, it is one thing to "teach according to the wisdom of the word, making reason the norm and root of the doctrine of faith, so that we accept or reject only what is accepted or rejected by reason; it is another to make use in our teaching of a wisdom that accepts, in the homage of faith, all that is found to be true in philosophical doctrines." Although we may slide easily from one to the other, a *foundation of authority* must be distinguished from *a foundation of support*. The Cross refuses to reason the prestige of the first without rejecting the services of the second. Philosophy does not measure faith; it offers its resources to it. It is not certain that the Greeks, our masters of wisdom, had pillaged the treasures of Moses. But all that is good, stolen property or not, belongs to God, who left us its free disposition. No risk then, under these conditions, "of evacuating the Cross of Christ."

2. The Cross will always be a scandal "by the unheard of things it proposes to us, such as the death of a God." In this respect, it is indeed the Cross of reason. Reason, even assumed in the light of faith, will always dread the illusory in anything supernatural proposed to it. This aspect cannot be overcome. Judgment can correct it; it cannot eliminate it. We must not conclude, however, that reason and philosophy are "enemies of God." Indeed, and above all, they tend toward knowing God and God's attributes by "starting from the world." Yet this difficult knowledge, contaminated with errors and inaccessible to most mortals, can become effective only if revelation, by the middle way of a popular pedagogy, remedies the uncertainties of reason. More precisely, faith assists reason to reach its end,

while remaining within the limits of its order. But revelation, in the strictest sense, opens the door to another order of truths, rightly beyond the reaches of understanding. Of course, human intelligence suspects the necessary possibility of this beyond; "the knowledge of the cause leaves in the soul the desire to elevate itself to the essence and innermost depths of that cause." It remains powerless, however, to transform this thought into authentic knowledge. The knowledge of faith fulfills the most profound nostalgia of the soul, leading it by way of obedience to its essential truth. The attentiveness of faith presupposes, therefore, the renunciation of self-sufficiency and by the same token the recognition of the Cross. Yet far from annihilating reason, this mortification brings it, by the boldness of a transgression, to the threshold of its true dwelling place.

3. These distinctions provide us with the elements of a correct exegesis of the "staurological" paradox. It is indeed true that for us the Cross is infirmity and folly. But this double negative must not lead us into error.

> Scripture customarily attributes negative predications to God, but it does so in order to signify thereby the excess of a super-abundance. The invisible is spoken of in this way because it is the most pure light; and this God, whose praise his creatures proclaim, is equally ineffable and unnameable. . . . In the same way the Apostle praises folly (of the Cross) in God because of what, in God, surpasses our reason by the supereminence of a wisdom that disconcerts us; seeing that we cannot understand, that is to say, fully realize the wisdom of God. But it is in this way that our reason is elevated to the divine truth, which is ineffable for us and which surpasses all human reason. (*In Librum Dionysii, De divinis nominibus*, edition Marietti, cap., lectio 1 n. 702)

Thus Aquinas interprets the negation that is so emphatic in Paul in the sense of eminence. The folly of God is really only the excess of a super-wisdom that disconcerts us in a first phase, only to elevate us subsequently to the mystery of the incomprehensible. That is why, in the final analysis, Christian revelation, far from being an abrupt rupture with the Greek and Jewish worlds that were its cradle, synthesizes all their riches. Analogy, which will later become the formulation in critical and semantic terms of a profound continuity despite a real discontinuity, expresses this optimism that transcends oppositions: wisdom and power "re-emerge" in God, that is, in the folly of the Cross, but within a world of sublimation that conserves what is positive in them and suppresses their limits. The final word of this paradoxical Scripture silences any scruple. To repeat a familiar expression, Greek and Jew, in their true grandeur, "become themselves," or realize their essences, in this Sign of contradiction in which "all is consummated." In this respect, the passage from non-faith to faith must be and can only be the passionate recognition (in the double sense of the word) of a realization, where each recovers, in the fullness of its truth, "what it was meant to be." No doubt, St. Thomas is not unaware of either the polytheistic meanderings of Greek mythology or the resulting uncertainties (within Hellenism) about such grave matters as the existence of the divinity or the universality of Providence. But confident as he was in the rectifications effected by the wisdom of the philosophers (Plato and Aristotle, in particular), he did not hesitate to welcome this heritage as "preparation for the Gospel," analogous, in the greatest dissimilitude, to the pre-Christian anticipations of the Old Testament. The Greek Logos, then, is not totally foreign to the Logos of the Cross. It enters into its texture, so long as some of its limits are set aside, particularly the tendency "to judge all doctrine by the single measure of human wisdom."

4. We might thus synthesize in a few clear propositions the Thomistic exegesis of the scandal of the Cross:

- Under the veil of infirmity and derision, the divine folly is but the excess of a wisdom that is an authentic attribute of the divine.
- Human wisdom, and philosophy in particular, has competence not only in "the things of the world" but also "in things divine." Wisdom and philosophy can be elevated by divine causality beyond nature, anticipating the transcendent mystery to which revelation alone has the key. Finally, under faith's guidance, they can illumine and defend the supernatural truths that a divinely instituted society has the mission to propose with authority.

- "Through this triple leap" toward divinity—spontaneous, philosophical, and theological—human reason participates in the
  divine wisdom. The distance between the two of them is less
  a matter of substance than of modality (finite on the one side,
  infinite on the other). It remains to the doctrine of analogy to
  give specificity to these relations of resemblance and dissimilarity.

- Because God is at once the author of nature and of grace, it
  would not do to have between the two wisdoms either contra-
  riety or contradiction. In virtue of the metaphysical principle
  which, in the hierarchy of being, subordinates the inferior to
  the superior, philosophical reason is naturally at the service of
  revelation. This condition of handmaiden responds to the most
  profound purposes of reason. And still further, the dependency that opens to it the oceanic gate of the divinity has sense
  or meaning only when a rigorous specificity is upheld.

- Image, by nature, of the very self of God, reason is thus "capable of God." Yet this near or distant capacity, because it con-
  ducts humans beyond the human, requires for its realization
  the hearing of a Word that solicits it without forcing it; the
  folly and scandal of the Cross recall precisely the necessity of
  this obedience. It would be a sophism to transpose into God's
  own self, in the form of a real contradiction that would destroy
  its being in sacrificing it to historical development, a "paradox
  which strictly speaking concerns only a mode of presentation."
  It would likewise be a sophism to reject a divine wisdom, or
  perhaps even every divine attribute, by interpreting literally
  the negative expressions whose meaning is normally understood in terms of super-eminence.

- Nothing, consequently, prevents the folly of the Cross from
  being an authentic knowledge of God that can subsequently
  be developed into speculative knowledge, since it awakens us
  to a higher dwelling place.

- What we say of reason, in its faithful obedience, applies
  equally in all domains. Whether it is a question of the Church
  or the political community, or of the moral or the theological,
  the relations of the human and the divine are defined by the
  same autonomy within dependency: by a hierarchy of beings,
  values, and significations that make our world a totally and
  strictly ordained whole.

- We can designate as "Christian humanism" a concept that accepts the determinations of this global order as principles of intelligibility and rules of conduct.

- According to this humanism, Christian faith is the religion par excellence, which fulfills all religion. In the same way, theology realizes philosophy and, by philosophy, all forms of human action, wisdom, and knowledge.

II. EXISTENTIAL EXEGESIS

To this Thomistic humanism, the Reformation offers a categorical denial, particularly in the voice of Bultmann. Over against Aquinas, it would underscore Cross rather than Logos in the expression *Logos Staurou*. The most significant text in this respect, *Glauben und Verstehen* (*Foi et Compréhension,* trans. A. Malet, Paris, 1965, I. pp. 517–563 and II, pp. 80–95) concerns the relations between humanism and Christianity.

1. Humanism, Bultmann specifies, is a faith in the spirit, in human nobility, in unseen values, in the community of persons. For Christianity, the world is a foreign reality. Christianity is a "de-worldification" (*Entweltlichung*) but without being an evasion." In other words: it is in the world without being of the world. It is important, however, to situate the disjunction precisely. Christianity and humanism have at least one thing in common: both protest "subjective desire" as an unconditional norm. Moreover, the Christian must not disparage humanism by dwelling enthusiastically on the latter's historical failures. And above all, the Christian will guard herself from the common error of reducing humanism to "strict immanentism," exclusive of all "theonomy" and transcendence. The distinction between Christianity and humanism "concerns their respective concepts of the beyond (*au-delà*)." For humanism, the beyond is a realm of the spirit that manifests itself in the world as formative power and the divine and mystical spark within. For Christianity, "the beyond of humanity is never in one as a gift, as germ or capacity or as idea." God is hidden transcendence, always yet to come, the perpetual future that can never be at one's disposal. The Christian life is a life starting from the fu-

ture, but linked to a decision in the present through which one is saved or lost. It seems to me that the guiding themes of this concept, which order the reading of Cross as Logos, are time and indisposability (*l'indisponible*). Without being rigorously logical, I will specify several elements of analysis, linking them as best I can.

2. We will posit as an interpretive principle the need to take seriously, in such a nuanced and critical text, the folly and infirmity it presents to us, without immediately compensating for them by rational strategies such as analogy. The text demands distancing from every power whatever: religion, wisdom, politics, or knowledge.

- Yet power consists in the control we have of *objects* through science and technology; of *humankind* through politics; of *God* through religion. And in turn this triple control ultimately presupposes that we are in control of ourselves. I am reminded here of the memorable definition of *free:* "To be free is to be the cause of oneself."
- The folly and infirmity of the Cross demand that we move beyond this regime of self-determination. Clearly, they tell us that we can not dispose of objects, of people, of God, or more fundamentally, of ourselves. In this respect, the Cross would be the radical critique of private property, in the broadest sense of the word *property*.
- Greek humanism, prototype of all successive humanisms in the West, is defined precisely as the affirmation of that power to dispose freely of things in the diverse domains we have mentioned. This power coincides with the ideal of the self, or the divine seed that we carry within us, or, rather, that we are. Despite appearances, mysticism is no exception. It is even, in a certain sense, the highest form of humanism.
- Yet perhaps Bultmann tempers his intransigence when he speaks of a "pre-understanding of God" that would be immanent to humans while allowing an interrogation, analogous to that of classical natural theology, because of the initial relation of the self to God. Such a hasty analogy would be a mistake. The interrogation in question, whether of God or the human self, must be interpreted as the possibility of being put in question by God, or of hearing from God a response that in no way

comes from us. This "interrogative piety" has nothing to do with a scientific questioning that involves the mastery of the object in question. In Bultmann, the expressions "human possibilities" and "possibilities of my own life" refer only to a power that is "obediential" in the etymological sense of the word, that is, completely at the disposition of God.

- If, under these conditions, philosophy is to allow for a "pre-understanding" of this kind, it must necessarily change its style, passing from the regime of the object and the categories that define the possibility of the object, to the regime of existence and the "existentials" that describe, in their organic correlation, the different ways by which human beings can be put to question by transcendence.

- It follows then, and I conclude with a play on the title of a celebrated work, that "Christianity is not a humanism." When I say "is not," it is not a matter simply of an absence, a privation, or a failure. There is no way to measure the chasm between these two grandeurs. Negation expresses an impossibility, immanent to the very essence of the thing, as expressed in the terms of Clarence Irving Lewis as strict implication. It also follows that the Christian faith is not and cannot be a religion, since all religion, which by definition is the power to dispose of God, is necessarily a humanism. This last conclusion has resounded loudly in the most diverse Christian milieux, Catholic as much as Protestant. We hear it from "Christian Marxists" who stress this incompatibility by relating religion to the fetish of consumerism. Whatever the relevance of this comparison, the exclusion that we have underscored is narrowly linked to Paul's sharp distinction between the folly of the Cross and Hellenism. The distinction becomes clearer if we add a new term to the preceding ones. We will say, then, that if religion "guarantees security to humankind," faith "calls humankind to renounce all security," whether this security derives from the power of religions, of science and technology, or politics. Seventeenth-century philosophy, I might add, seems to have been obsessed by two exigencies: scientific certitude (*certum*) and political security (*securum!*). In contrast, faith liberates us from this double obsession. "The Word of God calls out to humans in their insecurity and calls them to freedom, because they lose their freedom in their aspiration to security (*Jésus*, Paris, 1968, pp. 207–209). We note in this

text the line of formal implication that joins *indisposability,
insecurity,* and *freedom.*

- The indisposable God eludes the grasp of a philosophy that
would make the deity an object to contemplate or problema-
tize. There is, therefore, no natural knowledge of God from
natural theology. No category, not even that of causality, allows
us to lay hold of God by demonstration.
- To sum up the essence of the lesson of the Cross according to
Scripture, the Cross is the definitive judgment on all power,
and on all will to power as will for disposition. But the correlative of power is always the object as it "is there," under the
eye or under the hand. Faith participates in this judgment on
the world (in the anthropological and Johannine sense). Faith
is, therefore, the critique of the object, or more exactly the
critique of the God-object, as well as the critique of every enterprise that by the astuteness of its representations or concepts contaminates the starkness of the Cross and of faith with
the impure abundance of our human riches.

3. Religious humanism is thus to be seen in a new light. It is,
more precisely, the "worldification" or "objectification" of God.
The God of faith and of the Cross is neither an object that one
explains nor an object that one manipulates. Bultmann takes up
again, in this respect, the celebrated distinction between explanation *(Erklären)* and understanding *(Verstehen).* I will leave
aside the origin of this dichotomy, though ancient and reminiscent of Plato and Aristotle. What does it mean? "To understand
does not mean to explain rationally. . . . The mystery to which
faith pertains is related not to the nature of God's own self but
to the way in which God acts toward human beings. God is
mystery not for theoretical thought but for human desire and
projects" *(Jésus,* p. 210). If I understand Bultmann correctly,
mystery, according to the Catholic tradition, is above all speculative or theoretical. This notion implies a confusion between
explanation and understanding. It speaks, it is true, about this
subject, about incomprehensibility. But the true "divine com-
prehensibility is not situated on the level of theoretical thought,
but on that of personal existence." An example helps clarify the
matter. You cannot read a text about music if you are not a

musician. Exegesis presupposes that your personal relation to the content of a text provokes the question you address to the text and the response you receive (ibid., p. 117). The medievals, in another context, used to speak of "knowledge by connaturality." It seems that understanding also implies a personal affinity, a sort of connaturality, no longer with a nature or an object of the world, but with an existence, which always surprises us because it is always event *(Ereignis)* and always future. Let us retain this triad: *existence, event, future.* It is closely related to what has been said above.

4. This capital distinction between object, objectification, and objectivity on the one hand and existence, event, and future on the other, is constantly threatened by the temptation of "mythologization." Yet, if I may interject here, myth has two aspects. One, related to comprehension, is perfectly valid: it signifies that we "do not dispose of ourselves or ultimately of the world, because we are in the hands of a mysterious power that sustains us." In contrast, the second, deriving from explanation, no longer returns us to the God-existence but to God and the God-object. As A. Malet has remarked (*Bultmann*, Paris, 1968, p. 45), "existential meaning is perverted by an objectifying and rationalizing process which tries to master divinity by conceiving it as a being of this world." In its historical reality, myth mingles these two components inextricably. It confounds, if I may say so, the categories of existence and object. When it is taken up by dogmatic theology, it gives rise to meaningless propositions, that is to say, expressions which, under the guise of grammatical correctness, suffer from the material incoherence of the predicates in play, from a congenital malformation. In its pejorative sense, as in its theological recovery, myth speaks about existence in terms of object and about object in terms of existence. According to the well-known formula, "it objectifies the *au delà* within the *en-déçà.*" Or further, it makes of the transcendent existential an immanent object. Objectifying the "beyond" in the "here and now," it thus makes it a disposable reality. That is why religions speak to us of a God-man, of virginal conception, of sacraments or mysteries. In large part, the so-called revealed truths of the ecclesiastical tradition be-

long to this considerable corpus of religious representations. Faith is in continuity neither with revelation thus understood, nor, still less, with the speculative theology that explicates its meaning. Rather, it condemns it.

5. Still, the contamination of the "beyond" by the "here and now" has been rampant from the beginning, at the very heart of Christianity, in the writings of the New Testament. St. Paul, and above all St. John, opposed it vigorously. Today, faith must pursue the work of dispossession that the folly of the Cross inspired in these forerunners. To designate this necessary purification, Bultmann fabricated the barbaric term *Entmythologisierung*. Faith requires "demythologization," by reason of an exigency intrinsic to its own unfolding. In brief, it is a question of a self-critique that distinguishes the kerygmatic kernel of origins from the multiple clothings (images or concepts) that have successively recovered it from epoch to epoch. Can faith itself assure this radical discrimination? This delicate question might be resolved in this way: faith inspires the "demythologization," but the separation of the good wheat from the chaff presupposes a preparation, or in plain language a hermeneutical method, that interprets rather than eliminates mythological statements (*Jésus*, p. 192). Exegesis thus understood carries on, as essentially critical, the work "partially accomplished by S. Paul and radically by S. John, concerning resurrection and eschatology"(ibid., pp. 202–203). But once again, exegetical radicality is only the prolongation and realization of an imperative originating in the Cross itself. In this respect, the exegesis of Bultmann is distinguished from such exegetical rationalism as that of Spinoza. I am not sure that the distinction is obvious, if we consider not the contents retained but the intention which, on both sides, returns faith to its essence, beyond the representations given it. Although we might quibble about the last point, we must add a new condition that does not appear explicitly in Bultmann's text. The reading of Scripture, in the traditional understanding, was intended to support, with a reinforcing past preserved in a Church-institution, a faith that was deemed too fragile in individuals alone to resolve the problems before it. The founding texts invest this reality with an obvious social

importance. To persevere in being, the faithful had to confide themselves to a representation of God on earth, whose authority guided them "in all their ways." What's more, ecclesiastical maternity corresponded thus to a principle of conservation that would justify a proprietary right to the divine. This complacent possession of faith in and by the Church tended to efface the need for the initial decision, the one that situates us before God in the decision to be for or against, which must constantly be renewed. "I cannot found my faith as a possession. The eternity of God, as perpetual future, snatches human beings from anything that endures, any security or possession. That is why nothing can be described as Christian civilization, as Christian formulation. . . . What is Christian is always solely the decision of the moment" (*Jésus*, p. 93). Christian time is not without resemblance to discontinuous Cartesian time. Existentially, it is a succession of instants that follow one another but cannot snowball and agglomerate into a solid mass in which we might find repose.

If God is indisposable, the future unforeseeable, existence unobjectifiable, the absolute Thou who calls us into question, the entirely other who escapes the ruses of will and representation; in short, if God is indeed what the Word of the Cross tells us, then we must have the courage, in face of the Sign of contradiction, to posit the alternative that determines all of life: "Ultimately the 'either-or' of humanism and Christianity can be formulated as follows: it consists in knowing whether one is to live according to humanity's own resources (as spirit edifying the civilized realm according to ideas of the true, the good and the beautiful), according to one's own human essence, or if one wants to understand one's life as a historical life, finding its meaning in the decisions demanded by each encounter" (*Jésus*, p. 93).

This reading of the Cross, and of Christian faith according to the Cross, is presented as an exegesis of rupture, no longer in harmony with a Greek Logos whose summit would be Christianity, but with the decisive Word which, between heaven and earth, in the darkness of Good Friday, offers to each one the alternative of salvation or damnation. The theologian's very insistence here admirably reflects the radicality of an opposition that tolerates no middle term. When it articulates the dichotomies of existence and object, indisposability and power, future and establishment, history and nature, understanding and continuity, encounter and church, faith and religion, it repeats in each of us the urgent need to take a stand. It rejects every synthesis as a compromise unworthy of both sides. Faith is not a game of diplomacy that we entrust to the learned, that is, to theologians. Its radicality is no one's privilege. It is imposed upon the simple believer as well as the exegete.

That is why preaching itself, however popular it would be, must surmount, out of respect for this critical dimension, every fear of scandal that under the pretext of appeasing the orthodoxies too often converts into dogmas or first truths the fossilized remains of an antiquated mythology. The Word of the Cross appeals to the intrepidity of lucid faith, concerned with its own purification but also, and by way of it, with insertion in the very world of that by which it lives. But "how do we present the kerygma today without thereby making a vision of the world, whether in its scientific aspect or existential aspect, a decisive criteria?" (*Jésus*, p. 205). Is it possible to escape one pitfall without falling upon another obstacle?

More simply: How can we be in the world without being of the world?

To this aporetic question of yesterday, today, and forever, there is no readymade answer. If faith is never an acquisition or definitive possession, we must continually reinvent it. At least, let us be attentive to this final warning: "The Word of the Cross addresses itself to human beings in themselves, and not to their theoretical reason; to present it as irrational doctrine would be as erroneous as to present it as rational theory" (ibid.). We will have to keep this in mind.

III. Critical Remarks

The two examples of interpretation whose major themes I have traced illustrate well enough, at least for the Latin West, the contrasting images that give the Christian consciousness its proper specificity. As incompatible as they be, they revel in their conflict and thus betray the polemic unity of their destiny. I do not claim to reconcile them. I would like simply to reflect on this strange situation, measuring one and the other by the Cross they invoke.

1. To mark first the points of convergence, we note that both authors reject the simplistic interpretation of the paradox of the Cross as a condemnation of human enterprise. Of course, to respect the nuances, St. Thomas tends to bring power itself back to an expansion of wisdom, while Bultmann, through the mediation of the idea of "disposability," seems to effect an inverse reduction. But both understood well the grandeur of a "humanism" that must be addressed, because if faith calls it into question it poses no less a question to faith itself, so that faith cannot subsequently be rightly thought of without reference to its shadow. Therefore a double movement is needed, situating, successively, faith before philosophy and philosophy before faith. What, then, is faith for the philosopher?

It may be the popular and mythological expression of speculative or moral truths: from this perspective, there would be continuity between the two procedures, a substantial continuity under the diversity of modes. It might also be an ethical exigency of justice or interior conversion. Yet it is not excluded, as a third hypothesis, that it is resolved in emotional irrationality, centered on egocentric nostalgia for personal salvation. Conversely, philosophy arrays faith with different forms that correspond symmetrically to the preceding possibilities. At best, it assumes the dignity of a distant preparation for the Gospel. But more often, it is affirmed as a formidable rival: whether it offers a salvation that would render vain the mission of Christ, or whether it transcends itself in a mystical "transrationality" that judges all reason. Whatever perspective is adopted, there is an equal danger on both sides: we make faith a diminution or a degradation of philosophy, or we make philosophy the conceptual advancement of a presupposed religious content.

2. Our two theologians are careful, above all, to preserve the irreducibility of faith. But how they safeguard it depends on

how they understand the negative implied by the infirmity of the Cross. Because he interprets it in terms of eminence, Thomas Aquinas accentuates in the Logos all that this term evokes of the passion of a supreme wisdom, the reason for things and the meaning of history, and it would not occur to him to separate explanation and understanding, seeing that wisdom prepares them. Bultmann understands better the rupture with Hellenism. He refrains in consequence from translating Logos by reason. He remembers the biblical Word, so distant from all philosophy. But he does not forget that the Cross offers a new Word. Everything takes place, however, as if Paul in his declaration of independence was thinking only of the Greeks. Thus the two exegeses, oscillating from one pole to the other, seem to each retain only half, so to speak, of the integral difference.

It is remarkable, in fact, that nothing precise is said about the rupture with Judaism. I should certainly wish, along with Bultmann, that God be the indisposable, which no human ruse, wisdom, or power can capture. But the point of the text, it seems, concerns less our so-called power over God than the God of power who disposes sovereignly of the world. Likewise, one may rightly reject the God-object or super-object who gathers in the riches of transcendence all the perfections of the universe. But if we replace this God with a God-existence or an absolute Thou, having later to correct the psychologism of these designations under the modality of the "entirely other," we do not emerge from the sphere of contraries. The two theologies confront one another at the interior of the same genre, between opposing poles of object and existence, as if the rejection of the first implied necessarily the affirmation of the second. But the paradox of the Cross suggests or, more exactly, imposes, that we go beyond the alternative concretized by the figures of Greek and Jew. We have no right, in this dispute, to privilege one of these terms. The Cross opens another space, an "elsewhere" that cannot be articulated in either of these languages, even if, for reasons that we will indicate later, we can only speak them by turn. We are invited to a new exodus whose severity excludes both the reconciliation of opposites and the unilateral decision that privileges one of them. We willingly admit that this position is most uncomfortable. But it is precisely because this situation is as insecure as possible that, today as yesterday, the Word of the Cross retains that sharp edge that disconcerts us. It discredits our most learned or most moving denominations, whether we borrow them from an ontological vocabulary or an existential lexicon. The God of the Cross is also the Cross of language and in the same way the Cross of being, thought, and life.

3. Under these conditions, what becomes of the much discussed distinction between faith and religion? For this distinction to be perfectly clear, in our view, it must be placed again within the ensemble of dichotomies we listed above. It appears that faith is the unconditional recognition of the indisposable, while religion, with its entire cortege of representations and practices, is identified with a humanist technique of control applied not only to things but to the Absolute. This rigorous distinction, which recalls the opposition between existence and object, seems to me to verge on injustice and sectarianism. The "setting apart" of Christian faith as an exception leads ultimately to grouping all religious forms, however modest or prestigious they appear in history, within the same misunderstanding of God. We recall the Pharisee who renders thanks to the Lord for being unlike the rest. Would it then be arrogant to consider that we can recover in the language and practice of all religions, universal or not, something inalienable, an *inalienable part* reserved for the indisposable? Does not the language of negation, which is a universal trait, signify precisely that the God we invoke infinitely transcends all our ways of laying hold of the divine? Rather than reserving it to Christianity, I would enlarge, and even universalize, the category of faith. Faith would thus be the critical element within every religion that fulfills a reductive function on the objectifications and representations we need in order to reach out to the inaccessible. Objectification would thereby be a universal characteristic because the two functions, critical and mythopoetic, are related necessarily to one another. The first exercises itself, and can only exercise itself, if the second furnishes its "object." This complementarity comes into play, without possible exception, in both Christianity and in the non-Christian religions. It would thus be outrageous to turn

faith into an exclusive property. I do not deny for a moment the originality of Christian faith; an originality that is incontestable to the extent that it is defined by the Cross and solely by it. I would add that every religion in its way must practice faith. I merely reject, in the faith-religion opposition, the disjunction that opposes what is Christian to what is not. The true disjunction, at the interior of Christianity as at the interior of every religion, occurs between the indispensable critical function and the no less indispensable function of objectification. Bultmann knows better than anyone that demythologization is an infinite task that can no more be finished on Christian earth than under any other sky.

4. But perhaps I underestimate Bultmann's true intent. He does not repudiate, indeed, that which, in the Greek religion for example, contains homage to the unknown God. He knows perfectly well that we recover in other religions, Eastern in particular, the more or less elaborated rudiments of negative theology. But, he would add, that is not the issue, because he willingly agrees that the reduction of "images," "schemas," concepts, and representations in general belongs to a generally well-shared religious "common sense" that could be called the "reducer of anthropocentrism." He would agree above all that this common sense finds supreme perfection in the most refined forms of mysticism. Yet it is precisely this most favorable example, mysticism, that provides our exegete with the decisive confirmation of his opposition between faith and religion. Why? Because mysticism is the very triumph of religious humanism; triumph, because the mystic under the guise of modesty claims, by her own forces, to identify herself with God and thus appropriate the divine, which then becomes at the highest speculative level the possession of a purified intellect, realizing its power through this liberating purification.

5. The mysticism that Bultmann has in mind, which has indeed had considerable influence in the West, is well known under the name of Neoplatonism. Let us limit ourselves to this example, which is for us the richest teaching. In what sense would it be called a humanism? The qualification appears so strange that it must be looked at twice. I recognize that, even in

its Christian form, it has little enough relation to the Cross of Christ. Does it then follow that it has no awareness of the indisposable and must be classed with the efforts of the Titans to scale the heavens, or of Prometheus to steal fire? These images have a long life; they still haunt the kenotic hymn of the Epistle to the Philippians. They correspond perhaps to the higher will to power that has rent the human heart. And when mystical language speaks of union, even identity with God, it risks, if care is not taken, interpreting it in the sense of a mastery or a conquest. Nothing would be more erroneous than this amalgam, for two very simple reasons that seem to have escaped the historian's sagacity. On the one hand, the Good or the Principle, whose hold the mystic experiences, could not be the object of control or possession, because it is beyond both being and having. No attribute could qualify it, and that is why in the Middle Ages it was designated as "nothingness par excellence" or "uncreated nothingness." There cannot, then, be a question of possessing or conquering it, as if it disposed of an empire that would be, identical with its being, the infinity of perfections. On the other hand, and in a corresponding way, the Principle precedes, and from all eternity so to speak, the ascetic exercise of will and will itself. Mysticism thus presents itself as the radical critique of will and of power, in God as much as in humanity. The quietism for which it has been blamed is only the expression of this transcendence. So much so that, in the final analysis, nothing is more alien to mysticism than this "humanism" that it is alleged to exemplify. It is because humankind "infinitely outpasses humankind"; it is because will and possession are all too human; it is because being and having are only the all-too-human trace of an unnamed beyond, that the soul and its God become more equal in indisposability. Unity is effected, this side of all riches and conquest, in a sublime poverty or the "nakedness of all things." And it is thus, I would add without compromising eclecticism, that the God of the Cross is so close to the God of the mystics, however obvious the diversity of contexts. The exorbitant "equality" with which pantheism is charged is but the awareness of this poverty that forbids, on both sides, every increment of riches or property that would support the claim of a difference. The Logos of the Cross is doubtlessly more radical than a certain radicalism believes. The two interpretations on which I have commented, while of great interest in the history of the Christian theology of the Cross, are perhaps only two necessary and incompatible ways of failing to grasp its radicality.

3

The Fools of Christ

THE SECOND ASPECT of the Cross that has met with an unexpected development in history is designated in our text by the noun *Moria:* folly, excess, alienation. This term must be conjugated with the other term from Plato (not Paul) which, in the *Symposium, Phaedrus,* and *Ion,* denotes an outburst of love, inspiration, enthusiasm, and the reciprocal dwelling of God in the soul and the soul in God. "This madness," *Phaedrus* (244c) makes clear, "is a thing of beauty each time that by divine dispensation it is born." Plato distinguishes several forms of it. I will not belabor them. By way of introduction, I would prefer to take from that same dialogue a passage that describes well enough the Cross and those "fools of Christ" and whose exploits are recounted in the *Dictionnaire de Spiritualité* (s.v.).

> A human intelligence must be exercised according to what is called the *idea,* moving from a multiplicity of sensations toward a unity assembled by the act of reflection. Yet this action consists in a remembering of objects that our soul has seen in times past. . . . When it regards from above all that to which we attribute reality in our present existence, it lifts its head toward what is truly real. (249c., trans. by L. Robin, collection Budé)

I do not make these fools disciples of the Academy. Yet I deliberately apply to them the description of *Phaedrus,* so faithful it is to their experience. For they also have a single "idea" (that is why they are mad), with all that the word "idea" connotes of simplifying perspective, of reduction to that "One" to which we return unceasingly because we never cease leaving it. And they also are people of a distraught memory, of that essential past dominated by the Cross. They regard from on high, from the height of the Cross, "all that to which we attribute reality in our present existence." And they turn their heads toward that "Nothingness" that their faith shows them to be "worthy of being," because it is in and by this Nothingness that they are what they are: divine human beings whose folly carries them in a "metaphor" (in the etymological sense of the word) which makes them continually "transit" toward the Crucified, for it is there that their treasure and their heart repose. Yet the enthusiasm that seizes them has nothing to do with the antiquated and medieval "feast of fools" that has recently been revived in the West to compensate for the banality of everyday existence. We must not forget that these extravagants, even though they have roles in a "history of folly," are not unaware of their specificity. Like Paul (1 Cor. 5,10), they are "fools in the cause of Christ," repeating in their creative way that divine ecstasy that draws the divinity from the placid domain of ontology where it has been held captive by a certain tradition of philosopher-theologians. I will draw freely from the previously cited study consecrated to them. And I will try to extract the lesson of their adventure.

I. THE CALL OF THE BEATITUDES

1. These blessed ones, or these "living redeemed," have heard the call of the Beatitudes. They know that the world of faith is a "world overturned." They have already initiated in their lives a first reversal, since they were recruited, in Russia and the Orient, from monasticism. But they add to the traditional monastic renunciations the abdication of common sense. We sometimes reproach them for an overly explicit desire for eccentricity. This is their way of proclaiming themselves, in the name of the Cross, to be beyond and outside the law. Likewise, they seem to make fun of suffering, displaying a stoic insensibility regarding it. Beyond good and evil, they assess the relativity of public norms and commonly accepted values. The burning coals on which they march, the heavenly nudity that suffices to clothe them like the lilies of the field, the concert of savage beasts that incline themselves mysteriously before their poverty: so many signs of a return, for the sake of the Cross, to the first

sun of origins. Not even the prostitutes, with whom they love to dance, have in respect to them the providential mission of assessing their degree of indifference. They must, by every means, by shocking the sensibility, make felt the absolute novelty of the message that resounds in bodily contortions. The body is, in fact, so important that it seems to replace the spirit. These people, called "idiots" and "unlettered," thus hear the continued derision of the powers that attached Christ, long ago, to the wood of his supplication. But perhaps a more precise intention must be read in these disordered gesticulations that evoke the harmonious circle of the stars only from a great distance. It is not only a matter of descending toward an "ante-predicative" that underlies the evolutions of reflection or discursiveness. More profoundly, it is necessary to restore to "brother ass," discredited by the prestige of the spiritual, a sacred mission: to confound "what is," in the unfolding of its power, by the weakness of "what is not." Such was the choice of the incomprehensible God, whose admirable providence, instead of calculating the best return for the least expense, cast aside the most probable possibilities of ever succeeding. Strange logic, which makes fun of learned premises and doctors' hoods, to entrust to these fools, to these simple of spirit, to these "beasts," as they once were called, conclusions that are displayed rather than demonstrated, as if the depth of things only opened up to a "beyond" or a "this side of" the noetic and rational. The Lord came among his own and his own knew him not. Ulysses, at the end of his odyssey, was recognized only by his dog Argos, who had held out for a last glimpse, before dying, of this absent one returned. The body also speaks, a little like the beasts, to make understood that which it does not understand, but which passes through it and makes itself felt. It would provoke in this oblivious world the remembrance of the one thing necessary. And that is why it speaks, in words, of course, but also in uncoordinated bodily movements that correspond perfectly to incoherent discourse. The end to be attained requires this strange means. It is a matter, indeed, of calling into question the established order and the governing authorities. Nothing will be spared these established grandeurs: princes, sages, and scholars, but also the representatives of the ecclesiastical hierarchy whose hypocrisy, formalism, and immense vanity they denounce. The monks themselves are not spared who, as much as and perhaps more than the clerics, have betrayed the Gospel by which they glorify themselves. All institutions merit invectives from these vagabonds whom destitution makes strong and whose weakness is the best argument against the powerful. In contrast, they are at ease in their natural elements, in the midst of the poor in every sense of the word, that is to say, those "who do not exist according the world." They defend the widow, the orphan, the beggar, and the slave. They retain from the Gospel and the example of the Lord a certain weakness for prostitutes, who represent, at the bottom of the social ladder, the trash and scum of day-to-day existence. We suspect that evangelical generosity is not the only cause of their inclination. No doubt, a component of passion comes into play. We observe here and there some sexual excesses that seem not to have troubled these intrepid ones. Perhaps they give themselves these moments of relaxation in order to better illustrate the necessity of transgression. After all, the folly of the Cross has little tolerance for measure. And if the errant encounters the errant, the apologetic result is only better assured, since they aim, above all, to shatter a common sense too easily adapted to the obvious. In this divine comedy, the critical function of the fool is to dismantle "that which comes from the self." We are given to regret that religious and civil societies no longer give a choice place to these champions of extravagance. In the Russia of former times, each city, it seems, venerated its Fool of Christ or its Idiot. The official Church adapted itself badly to this strange sanctity, marking in its way the distance between the Gospel and the Institution.

2. Two traits to complete this sketch. These vagabonds who go out in the woods and fields reject every permanent dwelling place. They live nowhere, as if they are not of any time. Living utopias, they seem to meander between heaven and earth. Yet they are not rootless. They have their dwelling place elsewhere, in that hollow of the rock where the Cross beckons to them. It is also there that their joy dwells: a joy that does not await the parousia of the last day. Rather, they seem to have always inhab-

ited this unknown land, from which they depart and endlessly return because they have never truly left it. "Come and see," they seem to say. These nomads of the Cross, who rest their feet on the soil only to remove them at once, are not apostles in the usual sense of the word. They count more on an action of presence than on a will to conquer. Those whom they draw after them are attracted rather by the beatitude they radiate and whose place of passage they are. Did Christ not say, "When I will be lifted above the earth, I will attract all to me"?

3. The Christian West also had its fools of Christ. But in this Mediterranean milieu, whose natural warmth has been tempered by Roman law and ecclesiastical legislation, we are more mindful, it seems, of the "reality principle." The spirit that blows where it will is under closer surveillance. Nonetheless, it sows some grains of folly. We should be able, then, on closer observation, to find there the same permanent traits, leaving to the historian the care of appreciating the original modalities. We must, however, add a double clarification that is not a mere detail. On the one hand, the fools of Christ among us were often writers, spiritual persons who entrusted to writing what their Eastern brothers embodied dramaturgically. It is not unimportant to note in passing that the most reasonable of societies, the Company of Jesus, refers explicitly in its inceptive mandate to a paradoxical definition: "The Company of Jesus is a society of fools and of those who profess folly" (*Societas Jesu est Societas stultorum ac stultitiam profitentium*). But in this respect, no doubt, the case of Surin is more significant than the career of Suarez. This mystical poet, who lived in the density of the Cross, smashed his head against all the walls of the rational and reasonable. He crossed a threshold of difficult return. By inscribing in his work and existence the critique in action of our imprisoning limits, he reminded his order that reason itself comes from further and higher. He might have from taken from Louise of the Nothingness the title of an original nobility, because being itself was for him but the trace of that crucifying "elsewhere" to which he witnessed among us.

4. Among the elect of the Cross joined together by our admiration, one name comes spontaneously to speech, imposing it-

self on all by the exemplarity of the man it signifies. Francis of Assisi brings to mind at once the stigmata of Mt. Alverno and the *Canticle of the Sun*. In Francis, the exceptional is so perfectly controlled that it makes itself forgotten, as if in human guise there passed among us I know not what flower of the field. He moves so easily through the kingdom of nature and grace that the prominence that marks and distinguishes him is effaced immediately in the common wayfarer of our paths. The extraordinary, which cannot but flourish, takes on the allure of a song, where the elements—water, air, fire, and earth—dance through the canopy of heaven. That love which is not of this world, and that the Cross reduces to a question, dwells in stark silence, so respectful of our decisions. Ineffable to our learned discourse, that love passes without difficulty along our ways, as soon as a soul, intoxicated by its presence, lends it its lute to disappear. *Il Poverello* was right that the instrument must not be an obstacle. Like Paul, "he wishes to know nothing but Christ crucified." But that familiarity, so connatural, is unaware of the refinements of a learned ignorance. It means no less than that he "carries in his body the wounds" of his Lord. This is enough for his happiness, if such an unworthy word can be applied to that Mediterranean icon of the Beatitudes. We sometimes speak ironically of "the imitation of Christ," as if such repetition offended some dignity or autonomy of the human person. But what do these great words mean when ecstasy transforms our heavy substance into a pure relation that dissipates its support in the quiver of a wing?

Francis preached to the birds as simply as to people, as if he read on this earth and its faces of shadow and light the universal transparency of the Sign of contradiction. In the beauty of beings and their ephemeral consistency, he recognized that Nothingness which gave them the face that it had not. Would not the most beautiful gift be to make "to be" that which one has not and is not? In contrast with so many who strain their voices to shake the powers, he guards against shouting. Is not the Cross, with which he identifies himself, and that he therefore no longer need carry on his shoulders, the necessary and sufficient judgment?

II. Scandal, Theater, Folly

This brief recollection of a familiar enough history invites us to a new deepening of the scandal of the Cross. Scandal: it was that from the beginning. Is it scandal still? For it is not enough "to have texts," however venerable they be, that tell us of its folly. The spiritual personages whose actions we recall understood that Scripture is not enough; nor is discourse, whether learned or popular. There must be something that actualizes among us the paradox of former times. But certain Pauline texts (Cor. 3,18–19; Gal. 2,19 and 6,11–14) already trace a first and timid dramatization. They invite us to "folly" because the immoderation of divine love calls forth, in counterpart, the immoderation of a foolish love.

1. It is necessary to show, then, that "the world is crucified for me and I am crucified for the world." In other words, along the same ardent line, it is necessary to add "to the Passion of Christ that excess that it lacks" and that can only be given by an intrepid faith. If the word were not so equivocal, I would speak here of *representation,* on condition that it be understood as closely as possible to the theatrical meaning. And in fact, it is indeed "spectacle," a theater (which shows us God "such as he is not") that the fools of the East and West offer us. Yet it is a theater in which, as we have observed, the bodily conversion of the ineffable means infinitely more than discursive speech. That is why eccentricity and strangeness must be integrated into the feast of the precious blood. There flows from this reality a way of carrying oneself, that is, of "carrying one's body," that, for lack of a better word, we would call "staurological." This supplementary body that Christ "takes on from the faithful" is indeed a crucified body, of which that on the first Cross remains the exemplar. In giving up the spirit, Jesus diffused this breath into the world, and no one knows where it comes from or where it goes. Our fools take hold of it again, reincarnate it in somewhat animal "spirits," supplementing it with body rather than soul. In the theatrical performance of the Cross, we find again the equivalent of a schematization. The theory of the schematization here signifies that the moment of Calvary, its quasi-tempo-

ral reality, is but a first realization, however normative, of the universality of the Cross. This normativity, still abstract because of its spatial and temporal limits, requires for its realization an unlimited series of images that reflect, in living human flesh, an indefinite possibility for materialization. Images of Christ, these vagabonds of the Cross, reproduce the ideal prototype. More exactly, they pro-duce it in the world, on the stage and machinery of the world, to recall to those unaware of it the grace of this essential past. Must we then speak, according to a well-known expression, of a "theater of cruelty"? It is an equivocal expression that suggests, to the experts on our depths, their well-known implications. Would the actors of the drama have a morbid taste for "blood, for voluptuous pleasure and for death"? We can answer as we will. It can always be said indeed that by accenting their more or less disconcerting traits, these fools were probably perverted. Yet however plausible it be, an interpretation cannot exhaust the reality submitted to its questions. As for our spiritual personages, they think they have chosen the better part and it will not be taken from them. If they play their role in a drama that goes beyond them, requiring of the extras the plasticity of an inspired organism, they do not measure their success against that of acrobats. This is a play "heavy with reality" that weighs upon their fragile world. They believe in what they do, and that is what distinguishes them from comedians. No vivisection separates them from the reality of this re-presentation. Yet the comic aspect comes to the fore again when they ridicule the powers to proclaim to all the approaching death of this world's gods. This death of the gods becomes then the condition for the appearance of the hidden God, who is nothing of the names attributed to him because he has nailed them to the Cross. In this sense, and in this sense alone, can we speak of comedy.

2. In this theater of the Cross, then, we can distinguish two possible dimensions or, rather, two possible orientations, according to whether the accent is placed on *participation*, or, inversely, on *distance*. Participation itself has two forms. First, there is the stigmatic inscription in the flesh of the wounds of Christ, conceived and received as the supreme grace of a trans-

figuring configuration; the active "mortification" which, by in-
fectious enthusiasm, pushes the flagellants' procession toward
delirium. The second is more perplexing. We would like less of
an uproar, even if we attribute the excesses to a vitality that has
need of bloodletting. The first, as exemplified in *Il Poverello* of
Assisi, has long captured Western attention and inspired commentaries. Experts expound on the reality of the facts and their
probable causes. If we admit the phenomenon's authenticity by
excluding fraud, we remain free to choose the type of causality.
Thus the medievals attributed to the imagination a power that
some of the learned have preferred to refuse it. In a hierarchical
conception, where it enjoys a median position between the light
of an agent intellect and the materiality of sensory organs, nothing prevents it from being entrusted with the role of a mediator
or of a stage between the soul's enthusiasm and the body's ecstatic breaking open. Whatever hypothesis we adopt, we can
nonetheless see in this corporeal translation the expression and
influence of a faith that could not be satisfied with the simple
assertions of a creed. It needed a palpable verification, in some
"performative" sense, that would extend the Word of the Cross
into a word made flesh. Only then, by the appropriateness of
conformity, the fool of Christ realized the "form" of his Lord.
He lived "in him," "by him," and "for him." That prepositional
language, so forcibly permeating the Pauline lexicon, was no
longer "verbal," but written from then on in letters of blood.
And in this Christic exodus, where the privileged one would not
have known whether he was "in the body" or "out-of-the body,"
the faithful people contemplated their true God.

A theatrical show, it could be said. Without any doubt. And
that is why I am speaking of "theater" and of "dramatization."
But here the drama so totally engages its actor and, by spontaneous diffusion, even the spectator, that the representation
tends to dissolve in a vivifying presence in which all and each
are at the same time beneficiaries and witnesses.

3. In the theater of distance, such as instituted by the fools
of Christ, the "comic" is, obviously, at the foreground of the
stage. I distinguish two comic modalities, according to whether
the discursive character is dominant or recessive. In the latter

case, discourse is subordinated to mime and caricature. Imitation exaggerates features and gaits to recover by this exaggeration the internal logic of an attitude or comportment. It is no accident, then, that the frog makes itself as big as the ox. In this inflation we perceive the "must be," so to speak, of that which is, even if we have difficulty acknowledging the profound complicity of the eccentric image and reality. I willingly admit that Christianity was not the first to lay the powers open to ridicule. For every power harbors in itself (one would be tempted to say: in its essence) the necessary possibility of its own derision. Whether they want to or not, those who feign unbelief believe it more than they admit. In this respect, all authority assumes its own excessiveness. Why? Because as soon as we are situated in a hierarchy in which, as St. Thomas recalls, "the more and the less are expressed in relation to a maximum," we are as if swept along or breathed in by that supreme Being who is at once reason for being and principle of intelligibility. The prince is already king, whatever he says or does. His weakness can only suggest to him the needed passage to the limit. And it is precisely in this pretentious superlative that the caricaturing mimic finds his best food. The superlative, in our languages, is as much the sign of "the most real Being" as the index of a possible ridicule. It passes without transition from the sublime to the grotesque. Now for the Christian, the superlative has died on the Cross. It subsists only in the context of worldly values. But the new god can be spoken of only in the most everyday language: that of weakness, insignificance, unconditional service. We understand better, therefore, what brought on uncontrollable laughter in the comedy inspired by the Cross: the literally enormous distance between the true God who is Nothing and these diversely named principalities that share among themselves the empire of being. This is not to say that being, of itself, makes us laugh or smile: as far as I know, ontologies, classic nor new, have never meant to amuse. But being's totalizing tendency, which has been a temptation in the West, always risks calling down upon the dignities of every order that represents "the whole" the just punishment for their *hubris*. That burst of laughter that deflates the windbags and reduces them to their modest size may thus be a salutary exercise of faith. Nietzsche lacked perhaps that tiny bit of irony needed to observe it. The fool of the Cross does not let himself be duped by the quasi-axiomatic values that claim our gratitude or admiration. He knows or estimates in the light of the Cross what these grandeurs truly weigh. Resentment? Incapacity to understand? Why search so hard? Is it not enough to realize once and for all that the Cross is also and above all the practical critique of all apparent evidences, as they tend to be imposed in their social deployment? When our mimes turn the caps of the doctors into dunce caps, it is clear they are not passing sentence on science as a system of propositions. But we cannot conclude from this that science, as it exists, is really practiced and not simply conceptualized, that it is not part of the thrones and dominations. And the singular turn that the actor gives to the earthly establishment of kingdoms shows well that he does not attack the majesty of a capital abstraction. The farce where his fantasy is diverted amuses the public; but through the burlesque of masks and gestures, through these "circlings" within which they are trapped in their sufficiency (was not the circle in past times the symbol of happy totality and self-sufficiency?), a critique pierces through, insinuating itself in the rudest spirit and rejoining, under a game of grimaces, the very depth and novelty of faith. To those who would complain of facile jokes or crude comic babblings, we must reply that the intellectual observation of a contrast, however refined, cannot arouse the popular sanction of a great guffaw. It is necessary to give this opposition of the Nothing and the All, of the Cross and the Powers, the face and sensible qualities of eccentricity. The fools of Christ no doubt sinned by superabundance. But we must not forget that at the horizon of their theater it is always and ultimately the Cross, and the Cross alone, that pronounces judgment.

4. At the limit of comedy, though we could arrive at the same effect by gross exaggeration, we find another form of derision, one that is more in accord with the discourse and seriousness of the preacher. The divine folly is not absent from it. But it must be submitted to the constraints of discourse. At this level, which is not that of the theatrical stage, judgment falls from above.

The joke becomes more abstract. The free fantasy of improvised movements is no longer espoused. Rather, it is a matter of indicting from the bar of the tribunal those who from now on will be the accused and not the accusers. The themes are familiar. We need to merely dip into the writings of the New Testament. The hard sayings of the Gospel in respect to riches designate in advance the newly privileged. Saint Paul had spoken of the Powers. From here on they are given a more precise name, which distances them from the cosmological entities of a certain mythology. Invective can then bear upon a well-delineated whole. When rhetoric has disciplined invective, the folly of the Cross tempers its virulence in the same stroke. The kings themselves will have their preacher to divert themselves "in serious things," as they have their clown to distract them from boredom. Another world begins. Perhaps another destiny. We must hope that it will not be that of oblivion.

5. What should we retain from this dissonant history of the Christian folly of the Cross? It is tempting to reply: the strangeness of the eccentric. But eccentricity returns us to a de-centering, a displacement from the center for which the Crucified has already furnished a model. All those who have followed him have lived and verified the Pauline assertion, "It is no longer I who live but Christ who lives in me." Folly consists indeed in "being outside of the self" and alienated in that Other who becomes one's very depth. This ecstatic going out of the self, Plato's *Mania*, is also a reduction, a simplification that returns unceasingly from the world where it must live, to this sign, to this *Eidos* where it expires. A reduction, but also an anamnesis of the one thing necessary against the forces of oblivion. From that sublime point, as subtle as a mark of interrogation, where everything is gathered together, the ecstatic can then contemplate from on high what is and what does not merit to be, and above all that incredible God, beyond being and thought, who renders divine and perfect in the enthusiasm of the possessed the poor in spirit and in truth.

Such, in terms as Pauline as Platonic, would be the basic attitude that has moved the fools of Christ, in whatever variations of climate and temperament. These men have desired that their saying be indistinguishable from their profound doing. They are not content to assert, "I say to you that he died for us" with the same detachment as we say, "I say to you that it is hot." "I say to you" is equivalent to "I swear to you," and this oath is their very being, or more exactly, the reciprocal immanence of the soul to the place that attracts and transports it, and of Christ to his ecstatic servant. Basically, if we may look back on the course that religious language has taken, we would say that the spiritual person returns to an earlier form of religious expression that preceded dogmatic propositions ("God is this or that") and confessions of faith ("I believe that . . ."), to the language in which Christians expressed the élan of faith, that of "being towards," the original arrow of the "I believe in Christ."

From this first de-centering or displacement of the self proceeds the judgment on the world. It presupposes that we have reached another space, and that even though we are in the world we are no longer of the world, through the image of the Crucified who, "elevated above the earth, attracts all to himself." Everything takes place as if the "méontological" force of the Cross rendered it master, this side of all knowledge and technique, of that which carries here below a name of being. This is sovereign freedom, whose promise must be realized by the children of God.

This judgment, we must make clear, is not fixed in a consecrated formula, in a "self-contained proposition." It adopts, as we have seen, the gesticulations of the body and the resources of invective. In the example of Paul, it bears upon the two great forms of power: wisdom and might. To the little ones who hear it, it suggests the permanent possibility of a distance; to the authorities who dread it, it recalls the fragility of the oppressor and the impossibility of imprisoning the human soul in the ensemble of social relations. And thus, through the comic element that throws into relief the contrast between the exercise of power and the ideological representation that it gives itself, the strange pact that binds Christian freedom to utopian imagination is born or reborn. The established order is only one possibility among others; its very limits invite transgression toward an "elsewhere" that thought anticipates without moreover being able to replace it. We might ask, in this respect, if there is not a hidden link between *The Praise of Folly* of Erasmus and the *Utopia* of Thomas More: two contemporary works that liberate the meaning of what was said in earlier times in forms that were less literary and not as mindful of the future reader.

We would be mistaken, however, to limit the activity of our eccentrics to the order of judgment. We observe in them the care of others: the poor, the orphan, the widow, the lost women. By way of the Gospel, they thus rediscover the flame of the prophets of Israel. Yet it is above all the example of Christ that inspires their initiatives and their sure instinct of what the commandment of love must be. If that love tends toward that "which does not exist," I would say this is not so much because of resentment or impotence than it is, inversely, because far from "presupposing goodness in the beings that it loves, it forces itself to create it," and to produce it *ex nihilo,* out of nothing. I have no intention of rekindling here the quarrel of a few decades ago, which seems tedious today, that opposed the Greek *Eros* and the Christian *Agape*. But I must note the persistence of that evangelical thread, that admirable vision of beings and things "under the species of the annihilated God": "What you have done to the least of mine, it is I that you have done it to." A certain logic unites here practice and belief, works and faith.

6. Finally, without being exhaustive, I would like to highlight two particularities that have not been given sufficient attention. The fools of Christ are first the "wanderers" who, in imitation of the Son of Man, have no place to rest their heads. The Cross has dispossessed them of every home and establishment. Their wandering is their own way of being no longer themselves. The earth is a desert that they traverse because it cannot be the "home of which one disposes." From this comes a sort of exodic impatience that Surin later will express by the strange formula, "savage-wrecked-mad." Yet without a doubt more surprising is the way in which the interior beatitude that intoxicates these fools of Christ coincides with a sort of indefinable sadness in them. This "sadness without cause," to which M. De Certeau alludes in his admirable commentary on the *Garden of Earthly*

Delights of Hieronymus Bosch, is perhaps not without affinity with what Sophocles, in his *Ajax*, designates by the expression "divine malady" *(Theios Nosos)*, indissociable from the "divine folly" *(Theia Mania)*. From where does this sadness come, this sadness that seems to have no cause, and which Spinoza would exclude because it can only "diminish our power"? How might we reconcile it with that joy, that "internal burning of the soul" that exults in its God and knows itself "in God, of God, and towards God," as in the Johannine Word, but by way of the night of Calvary? I willingly agree that for our ecstatics, happiness "is at the beginning and not at the end." It is principle more than recompense for action. Then why this veil, this incomprehensible taste of ashes? The medievals questioned the coincidence in Christ of the agony, the beatific vision, the sorrow unto death. The sadness they spoke of was ultimately very comprehensible: it was based on the "presence of sufferings," in body and spirit, interior and exterior, that assailed the soul of the Savior in the hour of darkness. But here it is not a question of a determined sorrow, specified by this or that pain. It precedes, so to speak, all the adversities that have a name in our languages and discourse. We can, if we want to, call it "ontological." But we are hardly more advanced—unless one means to say in this way that sorrow "without cause" and without object is due to the sole fact "that there is something rather than nothing." Would this then be the nihilism, already ours, that would traverse, like a malevolent and subsisting flash, the happiness of the elect? That would indeed be impossible; and I guard myself from gratifying them with our torments, or making them say that being as being is the absolute evil. Yet the Nothingness par excellence, whose disconcerting image and sign they contemplate on the Cross, teaches them something else. Perhaps this: that the being of that which is, is the trace of a first distance that marks its exile from its origin. Would it perhaps have been better had the world never been born? Its birth is the fruit of a double boldness and a double risk: boldness of infinite love that allowed the forms of beings and of things to unfold in the autonomy of their configurations; boldness of human freedom that can turn around against its source, and accentuate, in a sort of negative gravitation, a constant difference. Distinction is thus, however magnificent, and St. Francis knew it, a permanent temptation. It is that shadow over the world that is seized, in the morning as at dusk, by the sadness of the saints. This is not to make it a malediction. But it takes into account that negative that cannot disappear, no more than the wounds of the Crucified could disappear after the Resurrection when they were bathed in light. It would have been better! Nostalgia for a happy state that the theologians once expressed by saying that "things, before the world came to be, lived in God of the very life of God." Remembrance of a paradise that would have been that of a pre-existence, or at least, if we exclude this debatable theology, that of non-distinction. It is on this ground of bitterness that the beauty of creation, in its ambivalence, becomes perceptible. It is that the Cross is everywhere, and that it traces upon everything that exists the separation of the day and the night. For this sorrow, so profoundly resonant with the destiny of the world, there is no remedy. The fools of the Cross have known the blessedness of those who weep. And who can never be totally consoled. Because there is no power, in heaven or on earth, which can close that wound in order to dull the pain, or still less cure it.

4

The Cross and the Powers

THE LAST TERM of the Pauline triad, *Dunamis,* or power, evokes several well known literary titles, such as *The Power and the Glory* and *The Triumph of the Cross,* not to forget the reference to it in the saying, *in hoc signo vinces,* sign and symbol of the Constantinian era.

These links, as tenuous as they first seem, are neither fortuitous nor innocent. Power leads to the victory or triumph that accompanies glory. Is this magnificent cortege well-suited to accompany the Cross? Must the Passion be read in terms of the Resurrection that actualizes and celebrates its virtue? Specious questions, to which we should distrust too rapid a solution.

Yesterday and today, the power of the Cross has been invoked under diverse titles. To dissipate any further ambiguity, I will distinguish carefully the two very heterogeneous, though not unrelated, domains in which this *Dunamis* makes itself felt. Briefly, I will speak first of the kerygmatic power of the Cross; then of its political power, susceptible in turn to diverse valorizations that can be discerned through a more precise analysis.

I. THE POWER OF THE KERYGMA

1. The substantive kerygma, retrieved in recent New Testament studies, designates the loud proclamation of the Good News by a herald committed to announcing the splendor of a joyful message that profoundly concerns his hearers. We must not, then, confound the Logos of the Cross and the kerygma of the Cross. The latter necessarily presupposes the former, lest it be empty and void of kerygma. In this respect, though translations of the term Logos are always risky, I am inclined to relate the Pauline Logos to the stoic *Lekton,* from which the Latins

derived *dictum*. What the kerygma announces is the saying *(dit)* of the Cross. I cannot discuss here the controversies surrounding the status of this *saying*. It can be specified through the following paraphrases: "the Thing *(la Chose)* that the Cross proposes," or again "the pro-position of the Cross," which is to say, more concretely, "the God revealed in Christ crucified." This "proposition in itself," however, exists effectively only under its mode of presentation. But there are, a priori, two possible modes of presentation. One, and it is the more original, is precisely the apostolic kerygma. The other, second or else secondary, that we analyzed above, appeals to scholarly procedures. It coincides with what was historically named "theology." It would have been better, from the beginning, to have spoken of "staurology." The question of the relation between these two approaches still arises. If we accept, as many do, that there is or must be a certain continuity, how can this relationship be understood? The familiar phenomenological pairings, "simple perception-clarifying perception" and "antepredicative-discursive reflexivity," have already served other uses. Bultmann's category, "existence-objectification," would perhaps be less far afield. I am not sure of their pertinence. Having expressed myself on this subject in another work, *Ecriture et Révélation*, I will not emphasize it here.

2. When we use Paul's vocabulary in speaking of power, we must then refer primordially to the Logos of the Cross as kerygma. The enigma is not thereby resolved. We must inquire into the nature of this force underlying preaching; and, above all, into its reality.

In any case, Paul seems to have had no doubt of its efficacy. How else can we understand how he glorified its transforming energy? Was he not himself the first "victim" of this impassioned speech? And his experience would abundantly confirm this basic conviction, which he never abandoned.

The nature of this power is less certain. Does it derive in the end from the prestige of a preacher whose contagious fervor inspires those attracted first by simple curiosity? The Acts of the Apostles (16,14) speaks of Lydia, a seller of purple cloth, "whose heart was opened by the Lord so that she became attached to the things that Paul had said." This is a simple illustration, among others, of an often repeated phenomenon; but in all fairness, it also brings to mind cases of resistance or failure. In this regard, Athens remains a memorable example of an encounter without effect. This would not surprise the theologian or exegete, who would say that the kerygma is not a force of nature that carries everyone along with it. Of course, but the question remains: Is kerygmatic power the function of relatively external factors, such as the personality of the Apostle? Or of yet more external elements, such as miracles, which, according to our narrative, "accompanied the word"? If so, what becomes of this *Dunamis* that Paul seems indeed to incorporate, so to speak, with the very Logos of the Cross? We must, then, search further for the secret of this power; even more so because the Apostle, anticipating our objections, decisively excludes from this *Dunamis* both the resources of rhetoric and the stimuli of wonder, leaving them, respectively, to "those who seek wisdom" and "those who demand signs." It is in its starkness, through the more or less transparent milieu of the messenger, that the Cross establishes its Reign.

3. We think, then, very naturally of the intervention of grace. Yet this, to be more interior, always risks appearing as a "nonsubsisting" flash of lightning or gust of wind, as brief as the *suddenly* that blinds us or turns us around. We do not easily leave behind the myths of exteriority and objectification. Some willingly fall back upon notions of the extension of the Word through a sacramental causality and further support their explanations with analytical philosophy that (as suggested by a well-known title, "How to do things with words") implies a transcendence of our rationalistic narrow-mindedness. This reference points less to a solution than to the need for greater depth. To keep from betraying this power of the Cross, which we always try to assimilate to one or another of our powers, we must remember that, according to the very thrust of the Pauline exhortation, it is neither a superior wisdom nor a restricting force of whatever order. It must not, then, be interpreted in terms of a revelation of transcendent truths, or through the image of an arbitrary sovereign disposing unconditionally of nature and

history. In the words of Paul himself, "its power is realized in weakness." This is a paradox, no doubt, but one from which we have no right to retract anything. Yet its weakness consists precisely in that it is nothing of what we would like it to be. Thus we must maintain it in this "nothingness," though under this miserable appearance it tells us the one thing we need know, or rather, not forget. It reminds us precisely that the one God we must seek inhabits none of the dwellings that we have prepared for him. That is why, as best we can express it, its disconcerting power finds expression in a Sign of contradiction; or better yet, in the quasi-nothingness of a mark of interrogation that calls into question what we are, what we have, and what we can do. Not, certainly, to deny reality, but to invite us to go beyond its inevitable fascination. A Hindu legend proposes that the firstborn of creation would be the mark of interrogation. Without denying the originality of Christianity, we can transpose to the Cross this singular condition.

The point of this interrogation reaches to greater depths. "Sharper than a two-edged sword," it cuts through the diverse strata of our multiform "establishment." Without lightning or thunder, it insinuates in our being the solitary doubt that must not leave it. It frees us from that which we hold most dear, from that past which is at once our "essence" and the crystallization of a will to conquer. Would not the truest freedom be that which frees us from our being, and from being as being? That is what the Logos of the Cross tells us, without violence, in this predication that should be its proclamation. But, let us remember, it is "a hard saying and who can bear it?" As Alain noted in his *Entretiens au bord de la mer* (Paris, 1949, p. 218):

> Priests are ministers of flesh who apply themselves to covering up the great refusal that they themselves teach. And all sermons are ambiguous? . . . From this come the illegitimate settlements and vile treatises denounced by the righter of wrongs. Thus the Cross is betrayed and by us all; but the sign remains and traces four equal angles over this oblique earth.

He adds: "Every power must be vanquished. It is the first work, and I suspect it is the only one." Would not the power of the

Cross, in its kerygmatic fullness, be definitively this judgment on all power?

II. From Kerygma to Power

The historical paradox of the Cross would then be the more or less radical effacement of this judgment, the subversive Word's passage through the glories of power. What a singular and entirely human inversion mingles the energy of faith with political strategies, by virtue of a social pact that guarantees the security of public respect to fragile Christian freedom! The history of this compromise has been often recounted, in condemnation as much as apology. We commonly speak of the Constantinian era to designate the age in which the Sign of contradiction became the state religion. But the name of the era usually refers to more than the interval of time assigned to it by the historian. It is used to designate a certain "spirit of the world" which tends (I mean, exactly, which tends) more than is reasonable to join "the obedience of faith" and submission to the prince, Cross and crusade, Christianism and Christianity, the expansive generosity of the message and the development of a will to conquer.

1. It is thus explained that the Cross no longer advances, as in times past, naked and questioning in the disquieting simplicity of the kerygma. Now constituted as Grandeur, it participates in the established order, and, primarily, as a criterion of civic identity. The shameful sign is now the sign of uncontested belonging. Anyone who does not bear it risks suspicion. Social necessities have thus transformed a principle of uncertainty into the "placid rule of law." It has been domesticated into a "thing" that one must hold in hand, and it matters to authorities that, as Alain notes, one can "pass through the thing to the spirit." This reification has a twofold consequence: the Cross that appears on banners exists finally with the obvious solidity of custom and tradition. Further, in its apparent immobility, it appears as the norm and first impetus of a "truly Christian country."

2. Further, in being incorporated for the first time in a society, the Cross establishes in the collective consciousness the

dearly acquired triumph of a first victory. It has vanquished the ancient order to establish the new. But, according to a timeless "common sense," the god of conquering armies must be superior to the god of the conquered. He is indeed the unique god whose unicity is affirmed and verified in the uprooting of the opponents. That is not yet all. For the superior is here the supreme, the maximum, and everything must be conceived in relation to it. Henceforth, its reign demands the universality of its domain, that is to say, submission to its values, called Christian or Western, throughout regions, near or far, whose difference demands assimilation. To give account of the new conquests, a facile theology explains without difficulty that obedience is, for the inferior, the only way to be free. Is the Christian faith not the truth to which all that is not Christian obscurely aspires in order to return to its essence? Extending its supremacy, the Cross suppresses difference only to restore each to its authentic identity. A society of universal law can thus repose in its shadow and taste, without realizing it, Spinoza's definition of "agreement with itself" (*l'acquiescence en soi*), "the joy that comes as humans contemplate their proper power." The folly and infirmity of origins are now no more than a bad memory.

3. The Cross that had once been "the beyond" of all wisdom and all power has been transmuted into the sufficient reason of a Christian world. Indeed, as if by a certain understanding of "theologico-political" relations, a society that invokes the divine cannot but participate in the apodicity of its god. It cannot be content with being: it implies necessarily an "ought to be" that requires its own realization. Because the "city of God" is the "city of the Good," it obeys a sort of ontological argument: Is it not to be expected that what merits *to be* should have the sanction of effectiveness forever? From this point on, there is nothing that prevents the legitimation, in the name of the Cross and its indispensable radiance, of practices that surprise or scandalize the Christian as much and even more than the "infidel." It would be tempting to go on deriding or abusing the political image of the Cross bequeathed to it by a certain historical contingency that adorned it with universal and eternal prestige. In

today's language, we would speak of "ideology," with all that the term denotes of justification, of nostalgia, and above all of admiration for strong regimes that are able to survive. The dubious exchange that renders to Christ crucified what belongs to Caesar, and to Caesar what belongs to Christ, would then have been only a bad calculation: the "victory of faith over the world" is sealed, in the final instance, by a victory of the world over faith.

4. This situational analysis, where the conflict that rends Christianity already pierces through it, would be incomplete and even unjust if I did not give those who call it into question the right to respond. The partisans of "the ancient order," or of "just order," would willingly remind us that we must not be dreamers. The "reality principle," applied to the Cross, simply means that the spiritual is not dissociated from the temporal. The Cross, they say, must be allowed to reign. But left to its nakedness between earth and heaven, it lacks its existence "in the world," and risks evaporating into shadowy inconsistency. It requires, for its existence, that "body of Christ" that is called the Church; but the Church itself can only unfold the virtues of its vocation in all dimensions if it animates, in turn, the social body, which it impregnates with its spirit and laws. It is not a matter of confounding domains, but only of refusing to separate them. Any vivisection would be fatal which, at risk of true schizophrenia, would divide the human universe into two juxtaposed substances. Christian common sense, too often misunderstood, is not wrong to invoke the harmony of differences that postulates both the autonomy of the differences and the just hierarchy of their diversities.

This obstinate realism, appearing as a sign of health, impresses again a faithful number who dread, in a certain understanding of faith, I know not what nocturnal passion of chaos. Truly, it is more shared than we think, even by those who, by virtue of their Christian worldview, combat the "dangerous liaisons," not to say fatal liaisons, that in their minds have compromised the Gospel with the injustices of power.

III. THE JUST ONE ON THE CROSS

For these Christians, revolted by the complicity of the Church
with a supposedly natural order, there is nothing mysterious
about the relation of the Cross to the political. They accept this
relation on principle. On the one hand, they can forget neither
the judgment of Christ "on the least among his own" nor the
prophetic tradition that Jesus exemplified. On the other hand,
they have learned from historic realism, considered as an authentic science, that class conflict is the major phenomenon and
primary inspiration of history. This struggle leaves no one indif-
ferent, the Christian no less than others. It impels an engagement which, for these generous ones, coincides with the very
commitment of their faith.

This joining of two apparently heterogeneous orders poses
a serious enough question that touches simultaneously on the
meaning of the Sign of contradiction and on a movement that
benefits greatly from a kind of uncontested obviousness. It
seems impossible to take a pertinent position here without having to understand, beyond simple elective affinities, what really
lies beneath the surge or the boldness of these more or less
controlled appellations. I will attempt here to construct the thesis of the whole, which underlies the options but has not yet
been laid out, as far as I know, in the ordered ensemble of a
true discourse.

1. At origin, and I have no doubt that it is a question of an
origin, "there is" *(il ya)* the judgment of the Cross. This judgment divides humanity in what would be, according to the etymology of *Krisis* translated again by the German *Ur-teil,* a
decision-separation: on the one hand, those who exist according
to the noble values of wisdom and power; on the other the
anonymous and undifferentiated ensemble of those who, by
reason of constraint and not of essence, do not accept these
values. But Christ pronounced himself without equivocation for
what does not exist. The God he invokes tolerates no wavering:
this God can be spoken of or affirmed through neither classical
philosophic categories nor in the traditional attributes discerned
by the religions.

2. This first division is closely related to a second, more modern, division which, like Bultmann but with a different spirit, places faith and religion in opposition. Both have been enveloped in the same unfortunate destiny by one of history's customary reversals: the revolution of freedom ending in the terror of dictatorship. It is urgent, therefore, to undo these malevolent solidarities, and to rediscover, beyond the ideologies of the Churches, the evangelical ferment of faith. By this critique, which effects the discrimination of elements, we must continually guard against the naive illusion that would discern by textual analysis alone a pure and indissoluble evangelical kernel. In reality, as the force of things or conditions go, contamination has been rampant since the beginning. We consequently relinquish the image of a simple body that the dream of a new alchemy would disengage under the sign of critique at the end of its effort. Authentic Christianity is not behind us: it is in front of us. But it is up to us to make it exist as fully as possible, according to its best tendency: that, precisely, which could not be imposed over the course of centuries.

3. This task of faith is of a *collective* nature. But how should we understand this adjective, called to such an extraordinary destiny? No doubt, the old Church understood very well that one does not save oneself alone. The very idea of *ecclesia,* in its most often exploited sense, rested, sometimes immeasurably, on the "system of social relations." However, and despite this ecclesiastical corrective, individualism has for a long time dominated the Christian conscience. The obsession with personal salvation, sometimes aggravated by psychologism or egocentrism, has relegated to the background a more noble concern which, in the right line of faith, used to expand to the dimensions of the world, a world that was above all that of the disinherited and little ones. It is well, then, that we reverse the natural or so-called natural movement that obliterated the imperative of a justice without boundaries in the name of a condescending charity.

This first reversal is of a capital importance. If one examines it closely, one observes that it carries with it some serious consequences. It implies not only that the individual is forgotten in

the "cause" that overtakes her. Instead of persisting as establishment, the Church must in the final analysis be forgotten in the
service of the poor, that is to say, in Paul's very language, in
unconditional devotion to "those who do not exist." And this
double mutation calls forth a third, which conditions the two
others. Until now, in effect, the major axiom that guided action
was summed up in the celebrated formula, "God first to be
served." All the energies of faith were, in consequence, polar-
ized on a Transcendence, on a sublime Object, to which they
rendered the homage of a liturgy of adoration, contemplative
prayer, and glorification. But if we hold that "God has died in
Jesus Christ," if in the name of faith and fidelity to the Cross
we reject the eminence of a supreme Being of which the religions have always been the more or less self-interested servants,
we can no longer maintain, in the name of the one thing necessary, the royal image of an Absolute draining to itself the living
forces of the human soul. At the very least, we can ask, according to the very logic of this thesis, if the word "God" can still
have meaning. We are tempted rather to pull down the religious
line of ascension and evasion to the temporal and earthly horizon. Christ on the Cross would then substitute for the Father
who is in heaven, but he would replace him only to efface himself in turn in the anonymous and suffering multitude. Of
course, the immortal word remains: "what you have done to one
of them, it is I to whom you do it." But this infirmity displays
no pretension to a separate existence. It disappears, in name
and in face, in the concrete universality of the "non-existent
class." The christological absolute is destined to the same death
as the theological absolute. What remains? Neither divine nor
human substance, but only a simple and impersonal function
that defines itself at once as transformative energy and exigency
of justice. The unconditioned, whatever be its form, is integrally
absorbed in the immanence and urgency of a task of liberation.

4. The Christian faith, as hermeneutic of the Cross, should
consequently oppose no resistance to the multiple instances
that may, on our earth, solicit its collaboration. Since it is not
knowledge in the strict sense of the word, it does not have to
concern itself with a Mystery par excellence that would exile it

from human truth. Distanced from interminable conflicts between science and faith, the Christian faith submits itself freely to a historical science that teaches it the precise conditions of an effective action. Better yet, since it need no longer live, as in Bultmann's understanding, an obedient existence that receives from the Indisposable the ever-acquired gift of its most profound freedom, nothing hinders its integration within a political project of "worldwide dimensions" that rejoins, in common concern for the exploited of every genre, the best of its hope. In the simplistic imagery of political language, let us say that if Christianity has too often leaned toward the right, it must now opt resolutely for its left hand.

5. Yet we realize that the thesis thus presented in rigorous abstraction is not necessarily shared, in all its elements, by all those who adhere to it or are inspired by it. It is appropriate, then, to note diverse hypotheses that contradict or qualify one or another of these elements. I will set forth these hypotheses, clarifying each time the essence of the *position*, the *decision* it implies, and the *presuppositions* underlying it. This scholarly clarity will put a little order in some often confusing debates.

The First Hypothesis

The first of these hypotheses is distinguished by theoretical and practical radicality.

POSITION

- The god of religions died on the Cross. This god is no longer of concern for Christian faith.
- Christ himself, stripped of the divine attributes with which traditional dogma clothed him, is no more than the necessity of his passage or death among in the multitude of the oppressed.
- The Cross, in the form of the "suffering servant," represents and signifies the imperative of justice and liberation.
- This liberation is really possible only by means of a worldwide organization that reflects in its universality the potential universality of faith and of a necessary struggle.

DECISION

- Since faith, in its ethical essence, requires a political engagement;
- and since, moreover, the efficacy of this engagement postulates both the theoretical regulation of an "historical science" and the rigorous discipline of a concerted action;
- it follows that Christians, by fidelity to the Cross in its primary meaning, must insert themselves in a party which is, adequate to the required conditions, the Party par excellence, already designated by a common language, without being named, by the majesty of a definite article.

PRESUPPOSITIONS AND POSTULATES

Presuppositions: These concern, on the one hand, the originality of the "Christian fact"; and on the other, the exceptional privilege one accords to a certain party.

Postulate 1: There can be no middle term between faith (Christian) and religion. Religion, however, is escape toward the illusory transcendence of an Object or a supreme Being. Faith, then, can find its support only in the temporal immanence of a "liberation" to be accomplished. The real content of a mythical "salvation" is, consequently, as we have come to understand, only the imperative of justice.

Postulate 2: The distinction between faith and revolutionary exigency is not of nature but of mode and degree. Of mode, because, in spite of the substantial unity of the two instances, the struggle that involves the Christian is inscribed within a tradition whose images and modalities have a very emotional coloration. Of degree, because the reference to a past, however prestigious, risks always, by the weight of reminiscences, distracting action from the urgencies of current developments and thus weakening the efficacy of decision.

Postulate 3: There is, since Marx, a "science of history" that has nothing to do with philosophies and theologies that have sacrificed causal explanation to the understanding of meaning. This science, although indefinitely perfectible, is still valid in its major theses, which enunciate laws, as valid and universal in their genre as the laws of gravity.

Postulate 4: The unity of science and practice is realized in a party that is at once the conscience or common sense and the organizing power of the oppressed class. In recognizing the need for such a party, Christians are not being sectarian partisans. They are only translating the Word of their faith into action.

The Second Hypothesis

The second hypothesis accepts the position that defines, in its statements, the radicalism of the first. It differs on one essential point: it challenges the decision reached in the fourth postulate. Nothing prescribes, according to its estimation, the monism of the party. Unity is necessary. But we cannot, without sophism, confound unity and unicity. Would not unicity be, in the final analysis, a theological a priori that transposes to the level of action a religious prejudice expressed in varied consecrated formulas: a sole God, a sole Christ, a sole Church? These regrettable reminiscences, even though unconscious, elicit an imperative, at least among the most aware: that of denouncing a facile slippage that burdens the plasticity of a function with corporal substance. The Christian faith, for its part, breathes uneasily in an organism that responds less to its evangelical élan than to a need for security, or, shall we say it clearly, to the need for a church.

The Third Hypothesis

In the third hypothesis, the critique that has been initiated continues and extends to the first propositions. If faith and the Cross are nothing more than what we say of them, it seems, indeed, that they can only disappear. Indeed, they can no longer be distinguished by nature from the movement of liberation. They represent but a moment of it, or an anticipation that doubtlessly merits our homage and recognition, but which, when the time has come (and it has indeed come) must cede to an authority that is better armed theoretically and practically to confront the problem of an authentic liberation. Clearly: faith would only have been a phase potentially transcended. Moreover, it would provide the "new forces of the morning" with only small change, precious but secondary. But, before these too facile reductions, our responsibility is to restore the essential originality of the faith. Of course, it is true that the God of religions died on the Cross. It is true that faith comports a dimension of justice. But must we infer, from the impossibility of every middle term between faith and religion (Postulate 1), that the first is exhausted, as is presupposed, in the temporal immanence of a transforming action? Fidelity to the Cross, let us not forget, must prolong the Judeo-Christian contestation of idols, of whatever nature they be. Every solution that presents itself as the sole solution revives among us the dogmatic idolatry of the unique and its sufficiency. The function of the Cross, under these conditions, consists in rejecting the new absolute that is proposed beneath the species of knowledge and action. In particular, it must exercise critical vigilance on every sociopolitical movement that keeps it from closing in upon itself. If we misunderstand this irreducible aspect, which is perhaps the better part of faith, that which will not be taken away, we risk, by the very name "Christian," falling either into a compulsive repetition of what seems to have been acquired for all time; or into an unconditional apologetic, or into the temptations of an apostolate of recruitment. We do not escape, for all that, an illusion of transcendence. But however debatable the God-Object of a certain theology or Bultmann's indisposable God-Existence, it remains no less that the "powerless power" of the Cross and of faith resists every will to immerse it totally in a certain historical evolution. Uncomfortable position, but authorized by the evangelical and Pauline instruction: to be in the world without being of the world; to make use of the world as if we used it not. Even if faith could no longer lean upon an Object or a transcendent existence, it would still have the right to the word; a word that nothing can prescribe and that awakens, or should awaken, in each of us that *non possumus* that in times past used to be the mark of Christian resistance against the powers imposing genuflection. This impossibility of "identifying" fully with anything we practice; this sort of irony, such a detached and smiling "I think" accompanying all our representations or projects, will always be suspect to those concerned with the need for permanent mobilization. No doubt they will see in it the dreaded return of an incorrigible skepticism. But they would then seriously misunderstand the liberty of faith and of the Cross. Because it is indeed true that we must engage ourselves in a transformation of the world, and that faith participates, and must participate, in the birth of a new earth. But the forms in which our labor is inscribed are but the provisional supports of an élan that comes from beyond ourselves. Fidelity to the Cross must join courageous commitment to struggles in the name of justice with that freedom of detachment that always refuses to take an oath.

This journey by way of hypotheses will help, I hope, to clarify a very muddled situation. Generous Christians who know not, or misunderstand, what they do may perhaps recognize and judge themselves in this journey. But beyond the topical case that invited this detour, analysis of the power of the Cross carries with it a higher lesson. For it is not simply a question of compiling an inventory of historic forms that provide a vague law of three estates. That trivial result would mask the essence that has been traced in filigree beneath the purely descriptive succession of historic forms. The kerygma remains the primordial power. It is that which roots the Christian in the Cross, which is his dwelling place. Apparently, this "dwelling in" does nothing; we might assimilate it to the zero element. Yet this repose, from which action draws its élan, determines what will be, that is, the effective possibility of a creation. What we have called the political dimension of the Cross describes, indeed, the passage from this Nothingness to the realization of a world. This being in the world, under the two complementary and contrasting figures of establishment and transformation, actualizes an exigency that responds better, in the second of its versions, to the call of the Just one on the Cross. Nevertheless, on both sides, the realist principle of efficacy exacerbates the danger of a permanent fascination with the work of our hands. The Pauline critique of this temptation reactivates a third power of the Cross, which we might designate as the "power of distancing or withdrawal." We cannot forget or exclude it without "rendering vain the Cross of Christ." This liaison of the three powers, in and by their reciprocal implication, defines the "staurological power," the dynamism of the Cross. Each is free to stress one or another of these moments. On one condition, however: that of not separating what analysis distinguishes and life must unite.

6. The problem of unity arises at another level, when we examine from this side of their realizations in time, the relation of the three great genres—*Logos, folly, power*—that our cursory phenomenology has sketched out. A chronological order is not adequate for grouping them, for they coexist in a same time and a same space. We can invoke, it is true, a dialectic of deficiency that condemns each one to its own excess. Thus the Logos of the Cross, in the very theologies that seek to match it, so disconcerts our wisest discourse that it always sows that seed of folly that nourished the fools of Christ. And folly itself would have been only a sweet madness if those who lived it had not suspected its strange power. A game of mediation that does not seem forced thus softens the rigidity of the forms. One might think of an internal pressure, a circulation of reciprocity remotely analogous to the Trinitarian dogma. But however plausible this relationship may be, it cannot dispense us from a reflection that is more attentive to the logical connection of the elements. It is this internal logic, and no longer its manifestation in Christian existence, that we must now restore.

5

The Logic of the Cross

THE PASSAGE from a phenomenology of attitudes to a logic of the Cross immediately encounters an impossibility. How do we still speak of "logic" in a domain that excludes, by definition, every reference to the most current meaning of this word? It seems that the two spheres will become heterogeneous only by way of malformed or meaningless expressions. This aporia is readily resolved if we distinguish between the Thing about which the Sign of contradiction speaks to us (and which is removed, as we shall see from the jurisdiction of Logos) and the Sign of contradiction as it figures in discourse, particularly the Pauline discourse. Yet this discourse, which we use as a basis, makes use of terms or linguistic symbols such as *Logos, Moria,* and *Dunamis,* which are supposed to express something, to have a meaning that is not arbitrary, to be related within a structure or configuration independent of the acts or attitudes historically and psychologically determined by the discourse. We understand by the "logic of the Cross," in a particular sense here, this structure itself; and, by extension, the reflection we are developing on the subject. I leave to the experts the concern over whether such an enterprise derives from applied logic, or, more especially, from the "logic of religion."

I. THE WRITTEN *(L'ÉCRIT)* AND ITS "MEANING" *(DIT)*

1. What matters essentially, however, is that we take the measure of a text. When Paul declares, in a certain milieu, "The Logos, that of the Cross, is folly for those who are lost, but for those who are saved, it is power of God," he joins, in an indicative proposition that stigmatizes any compromise, the descriptive properties of a certain "singularity." The originality of the

message does not exempt it from the generic conditions to which every human intention is submitted. To have an impact on the world, the Cross must manifest itself in an intelligible and communicable "meaning," however diverse be its modes of presentation. The semantic content that the predication yields is affected by a double reference: it is addressed to all, at least in principle, without ethnic or religious discrimination; the intentionality *(vouloir dire)* that it incorporates refers to the event of the Cross and, by way of that event, to the coming of the new god in the darkness of absolute infirmity. The Apostle does not detail the elements of the kerygma that mission or catechesis aimed to explicate, and which he sums up in two words: Christ crucified. But he indicates clearly, in a second language (or metalanguage), the characteristics of his discourse. And he joins it to the three memorable substantives, *Logos, Moria,* and *Dunamis,* which seem to have been dictated by the very Thing of which they speak. Paraphrasing the translation, one might indicate the movement of the text as follows: "The Logos of the Cross is indeed a logos, a saying: but this saying disconcerts our thoughts to the point that it can only be folly; and it is as folly that it is power of God." This seems to be the most probable content of the Pauline proposition.

2. Of the many permutations that might be taken, I will retain only the original sequence—*Logos, Moria, Dunamis*—which would be, in the present case, the nonexistent *(nulle)* permutation. Other configurations are no doubt interesting. Yet the initial order conforms so well to the original élan that I will simply respect it.

In the series thus presented, where each of the terms is irreplaceable in position as in function, I would be inclined to read a quasi-syllogism:

> The folly (of the Cross) is power of God.
> The Logos (of the Cross) is folly.
> The Logos (of the Cross) is power of God.

I risk this formulation, which probably clarifies little, for the sake of focus. I will substitute for it some more fluid expressions:

- the Logos of the Cross, as folly, is power of God
- the Logos of the Cross, because it is folly, is power of God

- the proposition "the Logos of the Cross is folly" implies strictly the proposition "the Logos of the Cross is power of God"

The first of these formulas utilizes the professorial *quatenus* of the medievals, which figured already in the "being as being" of Aristotelian metaphysics. The power of God is linked to the Logos of the Cross insofar as it is folly and not insofar as it is being. What does this strange particle signify?

To understand it, we recall that the staurological Word, more exactly the thing that Paul speaks about in a human language (without disdaining grammar, and resorting moreover to propositions of monadic predicate), carries with it theoretically an open list of qualifiers. From this field of possibilities, Paul has chosen the most adequate characteristic. He has therefore isolated it because of its importance. But this privilege could not be translated by a simple conjunction: "The Word of the Cross is Logos *and* it is also folly and it is power of God." The expression "insofar as" *(en tant que)* underscores precisely, by deliberate choice, the value of a determination that takes into account, in the name of necessary and sufficient condition, an other determination. In plain language, folly, in its mediating function (that inverts, in our syllogism, the position of middle term), explains that reason which makes of the Logos of the Cross a "power of God." There is a necessary relation, or rather what was formerly called a formal "implication." The formal implication, as the epithet indicates, underscores the connection of two forms, a connection founded on their very essence. In this relation, however, folly exercises a function that cannot be allocated an other factor: it is at once the cause and reason of power. That is what our second statement underscores: the conjunction "because" throws into relief the hierarchical and dynamic order that subordinates power to folly. By thus restoring the deeper structure concealed by the superficial structure of the Pauline phrase, we are not simply playing a little game of transformations. We are avoiding the reductive interpretation that in concern for literalness would evacuate an imperious "intentionality" *(vouloir-dire)*, difficult to reconcile with a juxtaposition of predicates.

3. Our third formula can be read in two ways. Either (and this would perhaps be the most common version) the Pauline statement is equivalent to this: "If the Logos of the Cross is folly, then it is also necessarily, and by the very fact, power-of-God." Or, taking in turn each of the two propositions, "The Logos of the Cross is folly" and "The Logos of the Cross is power-of-God," we establish between them, by an operator of necessity ("it is necessary that, if . . . then . . ."), a relation of strict implication whose rigor forbids the possibility of simultaneously having the position of the first and the negation of the second. However the two forms of modality differ, the intended meaning here would seem to me to be the same: the link that unites folly and power in the Logos of the Cross overflows the contingency of a fact of pure coexistence. Not only "it is thus," but "it is necessary that it be thus."

At the point where these explications converge, the "staurological" proposition attains the paroxysm of scandal, and the question becomes more pressing: How can folly, that is to say, the absence of reason, be converted into the reason and source of a power?

II. The Shadow of Scandal

The response requires a detour that is neither a digression nor a diplomatic ruse. For we must adhere to that which Paul so energetically asserts: the new god, signaled by the Sign of contradiction reflected in the Logos of the Cross, is manifested to us in the destitution of infirmity and folly, as if he had chosen this double "nothingness" to attract all to itself. How can anything arise from this nothingness? Such an aporia defies understanding. Where, then, is this scandal situated?

1. According to a most familiar expression, "nothing can give what it does not possess." The cause, we used to add in the past, "produces an effect similar to itself," which pre-exists at its origin under the form of idea and generative energy. In this respect, all "production" resolves itself in "re-production." Of course, when it is a question of God, classical theology main-

tains the distances. Yet even though theologians were mindful of the need to preserve transcendence, the biological image of causality imposed a corrective of similarity to attenuate difference. It has always been difficult to keep in balance these two postulates whose unity was problematic! The religious conscience adopts the middle way of that correct milieu. Yet more exigent spirits have always borne witness to a reticence of judgment and attitude that inspired simultaneously a more austere piety and a thought less beholden to the obvious. Of course, the god who raises us beyond ourselves can pass among us only on the paths of humanity. This god must be incarnated in our languages, as in our behaviors. It does not follow that we had to be duped by our limits. Here again, a need acknowledged is transformed into freedom. By detaching itself from its too human possessions, the soul frees its god in the same movement from its private properties. That which was attributed to the divinity by a sumptuous language is henceforth effaced in a smoke of incense praising the inaccessible. For the litany of excellences is substituted the language of the desert, which is also that of our exile and purification. It is in light of the function of this new spirit that we can understand the scandalous expressions "Uncreated Nothingness" and "Nothingness par excellence," which enchanted the tranquil courage of our fathers.

2. It has sometimes been thought that this quasi-morbid predilection for the negative failed to escape contradiction because, pushed to the extreme, the "rage" for negation no longer spares the negative properties (such as "not-wise being"), and that, as Bochenski observes (*The Logic of Religion*, New York, 1965, p. 111 s.v.), it is condemned, by virtue of the law of double negation, to restore the positive that it excludes. In reality, as demonstrated by the paradoxical expressions cited, our masters were victims of neither negation nor affirmation. These two complementary modes, which flourish in our discourse, must be equally transcended, for the one necessary thing sought by us eludes the multiple means it has given us to reach out to it. Yet since possession fascinates more than privation, the spiritual have focused on the positive, seeking to dissolve its prestige. The emphasis on "non-being" has no other meaning. It does

not redouble itself in a negative ontology. Far from betraying I know not what pathology, "the beyond of being" sensitizes us to that marvelous upsurge recalled in the vocabulary of the "orient" and "origin." If all had already been inscribed in the attributes of God or the divine ideas, the novelty of the world would be only the reduplication of an anterior that would contain at maximal intensity the richness of various stages, whose "subsisting light" is dispersed and degraded in our universe. Thus placed again in its context, the paradox of the *Nothing* opens the magnificent horizon on which and from which every being that truly merits its name will have "to make itself what it is." The power to make and to "make oneself" is thus always derived. It can only be homage endlessly renewed to That by which "there is something rather than nothing." The donative instance does not give what it has: it allows that which is to "give to itself" what it is.

3. These preliminaries, which allow the Pauline text to be situated against a larger horizon, in no way diminish its percussive force. They seem to me to illuminate certain aspects of it. But if it is useful to enlarge the perspective, it would be wrong to minimize the differences.

The *theologia crucis,* such as Paul exposes it in his *praeclarum theorema,* is of an entirely other order than so-called negative theology. It implies neither the subtle reduction of concepts nor the scholarly critique of our no less scholarly ontologies. It gives rise to thought, but by a sign that carries us away from the "region of resemblance" toward another space that is no longer, according to Paul, that of the familiar religions, of Greece or Israel. Under the images of weakness and folly, something is said that cannot be forgotten. The Word on the Cross has been freed by the sublime poverty in which it was suspended from any past of substance and possession.

Classical theology, it is true, was not unaware of the language of the nothing *(rien)* or the *nihil.* Yet without reexamining the more or less traditional classifications of our diverse interpretations, the *nothing* of which classical theology speaks in the expression *ex nihilo* refers to the dogma of creation in order to eliminate from it any artificial representation of presupposed material and a demiurge-creator. Despite this corrective, the image of the artisan remains no less dominant, since the creator carries out the operation in an exemplary ideality and finality whose convergence eliminates chance. And in any case, the *nothing* in question affects, so to speak, only the substrata of production. On the other hand, in the theology of the Cross, it reascends the mount of the divinity to exclude from it the metaphysical flowering that was often the contemplative's "garden of delights." Paul expressly names the major attributes of wisdom and power which, in the two types of religion he recalls, open the oceanic gate of the Absolute. These two excellences express all the riches of God, because in them and by them we understand the series for which they are, respectively, the generative monad. In this sense, they have the value of the indicative, although the Apostle had neither the intention nor the means (as would Thomism later, through the *esse subsistans*) to deduce from them the fullness of perfections. That is not all. Wisdom and power determine not only the "being of God." They are for the faithful the light by which to apprehend all that belongs to the divine sphere. Perhaps it might even be proposed that the mode of presentation founds the ontological attribution. We can measure from this point the importance of the reversal operated by the Cross. The God of Jesus Christ is offered to us under entirely different appearances. This God rejects the denominations spelled out by the piety of adoration; or, in a scholarly mode, by a theology inspired by the ontology of transcendentals. The Cross turns us away from a full and magnificent being whose spirit would be the hypostasis of having. It is from this height that the *Nothing* of which we speak inserts its burning edge, to trace the sign of contradiction upon the "most real being" of the religions and philosophers.

4. This first exercise, flowing most obviously from our text, calls forth in consequence some new exclusions. The beyond of wisdom can also be the beyond of the idea. In the same way, what we link to that prestigious term—absolute of knowledge, priority of the model, primacy of the end—is effaced in the new heaven. That which is "God's folly" tolerates neither the disposition of a universe ordained to its Glory, nor the calcula-

tion of maximum return for the minimum of expense, whether in architecture or economy. This theological space has a name in our Scriptures. It is the name of Love or Agape. Groundless Love, because not only, as observed by St. Thomas, "it presupposes in creatures no prior goodness since it renders them possible," but also because it rests upon no reason which, directly or indirectly, would bend it to any interest, however noble.

Moreover, if so pure a love defies all wisdom, it puts up little better with power. Its folly has, as its dispensable complement, its "infirmity." Unlike the despot who would reign only by reducing his "subjects" to the condition of defective modes of his excellence or docile instruments of his power, the reign of Agape imposes on its faithful no likeness of repetition. The god of the Cross has no other action than his presence, which prescribes no pre-established model but which allows each, on the ground of non-being, to become itself. It is in this way, to use a very human example, that if the professor demands, too often, alas, that his disciple repeat what he says, the master, inversely, diffuses around himself a space of freedom in which the listeners can inscribe the original form of a freedom that has never yet been known. The power that originates in the Logos of the Cross is less that of an all-powerful Creator, vivifying his creatures, than it is the dynamism of a faith that knows "where its confidence reposes."

These degrees of a divine hierarchy of the Cross, which we have reviewed as best we could, express the diverse "powers" of the Cross. From our perspective, these powers are exponents of an unlimited dispossession. If we may borrow an image from an absolute asceticism, it suggests to us that fourfold nothingness—of being, idea, motivation, and power—that puts a question to us from us from that tranquil height inhabited by the Sign of contradiction. Divine Word, but too hard a word not to waken immediately the multiform objections of a clear and precise intelligence, against the apparently disastrous consequences of such a logic of the Cross. The most pressing argumentation is based, indeed, on solid common sense: "The ascetic god we are talking about exists or does not exist. If he exists, he must have some determination. But it seems that he has none. Therefore, he does not exist." In its exuberance of attributes, the God of religions at least responded to the dream of a summer night brilliant with stars. The one of the new faith is but the bloodless result of a dreadful nightmare.

5. I will not enter into ontological discussions. I will retain, however, the principle we must keep in mind. Existence *(exister)* is not dissociated from a certain essence, if that word is understood as either a fundamental determination or an ordained ensemble of determinations or properties. Such a definition can only exclude from existence a supposed "beyond of being." Does it follow that it vanishes into a chimera, into non-meaning, or even that it returns to the absurdity of the ancient first matter that is "nothing of that by which being is defined"? It is so much more plausible that the god, from whom the last drop of blood was drawn, overturns the *object* in the neatness of its contours as much as *existence* in Bultmann's sense. What remains, then, after such a mortal subtraction? Not even an "almost nothing," but nothing, pure and simple. This evidence, irrefutable in its way, shows how hard it is to go beyond the representation of the object, as it is imposed on everyday perceptions or concepts. Would it be foolhardy to recall that today's most scrupulous physics contests that primacy of the object? It also impugns those images, tailored to common sense, assumed by a less refined science and still propagated by pseudo-science. For it is a question of that which in its austere language is less a "thing," whose face is traced by the eye or the hand, than that "by which" there are things and objects in our macroscopic world. Inadequate indication, but precious, perhaps because it prolongs the ancient distinction between the cause that "operates by likeness" and the principle, more difficult to grasp if not by "prepositional" circumlocutions: "that by which something is, or becomes, or is known." This more or less awkward detour passes through the slenderest elements of language to avoid what might be called the reflux of consecrated images and, in the same way, the danger of a reification. It is a detour most often accompanied by a negative explanation: "that by which there is something is nothing of that which proceeds from it." The personal sign in the pronominal expression would equally

go too far because it personifies what must not be reified. It
must be expressed at least badly, if not for the best. But this
critical vigilance, which makes every language fluid in order to
avoid becoming its victim, betrays already, in its dispossession,
the liberating presence of that which it seeks to take sight of. In
these brief sketches, by approaching the Cross through the Sign
of contradiction, I am not claiming to do metaphysics. I am
noting convergences that suggest a possible transcending of
what has been commonly received, turning us back to the soul's
barren summit, where the night wind of freedom rings.

6. Yet I doubt that these explications are satisfactory. In raising the Cross above the world and being, and faith above religion (which is always, more or less, religion of the God-Cause),
do we not once more risk ending at the void (at that *nihil*, whose
etymology is so telling: "not even an anything *[hile]*")? Is it possible to play with words as if the God invoked by the Christian
passed through our languages only as the impossibility of being
fixed there, or as if this passage condemns them to a perpetual
trembling? If God offered nothing we could grasp in our attempts to name him, could we still reach out to him? Faith
would be no more than desert silence. But let us admit, with
Meister Eckhart and many others before him, that God is unutterable. The Unutterable would then be God's name. The infer-
nal machine that makes a void in God and in us would itself
hate the void, since, at the end of the journey, it gives us back a
divine name.

Bochenski, little suspect of sympathy with the ineffable, has
recently done justice to this ancient objection that is always
being revived. Nothing prevents us from allowing, he clarifies
(op.cit. pp. 31–34), in a metalanguage of the first degree, that a
certain object (that of religious discourse) can be spoken in any
one of the languages belonging to the class of language objects.
There would be inconsistency only if we confounded language
and metalanguage. But this is not the case: "unutterable" as
"name" does not signify a perfection or determination analogous to the divine attributes treated in traditional theological
discourse; nor does it signify a negative property also susceptible to a "transcendent usage." The reproach of contradiction,

unjustified on the level of logic, would rather betray ignorance of the question.

Yet it may be asked if the Pauline text commented upon by us in the first chapter does not suggest, under the terms of "folly" and "infirmity," a sublimating transposition that would be, in God, the apotheosis of the negative. This strange exegesis, which I must entertain only out of fairness, would misconstrue the most obvious meaning of the passage. What the Apostle insists upon is the impossibility of uttering, in any language-object (of Jew or Greek, for example), that which we cannot put at our disposition, the "Thing" to which his heart clings. He does not, by a sort of inversion, mean to substitute, for the consecrated excellences of wisdom and power, their contrary correlatives. If such were his intention, he would also remain prisoner of the same propositional context of reference and meaning, despite the corrective of negation that he assumes for his part. We know, of course, that two contradictory propositions must bear on the same statement. But, the essence, for Paul, consists in a distance taken, in a change of level that is at once metalanguage and "reflective judgment" on what has heretofore "been said." Negation does not, then, aim at the constitution of other divine attributes that would reverse the first. It expresses the necessity of a mutation of attitude that remains incomprehensible to common sense. The Pauline challenge thus reflects the Sign of contradiction, which is expressed, in its turn, in the Logos of the Cross. "Folly," we note, affects uniquely the "saying" whose diffusion the kerygma assures. But in qualifying this staurological discourse, it pronounces the decisive judgment upon the "ontological" discourses of the religions, stripping them of their pretensions.

7. If such is indeed the import of the Logos of the Cross, must we not fear being hurled at a new difficulty, less subtle no doubt, but closer to everyday realities? It is a fact, some will object, that the creeds in which Christian faith is affirmed tell us well and truly, and in an object language, what is and must be the God of our prayer and our faith. No doubt the everyday or scholarly language of the faithful comports an impressive number of indicative propositions, which articulate distinct at-

tributes. Moreover, the very excellence that draws forth adoration and awe presupposes, in the One addressed, something other and more than a simple "ineffability" (op.cit. p. 36). Is it not right to take account of them?

III. The Cross of Discourse and the Discourse of Faith

It would be foolish for us to minimize or evade these very sensible observations. They must provoke questions whose timeliness escapes no one. We would agree, without difficulty, that faith has need of a creed that gives it a body of propositions. But the problem is less simple than it seems, because the creed itself implies a multiplicity of dimensions that must be distinguished.

1. In the innocence of its fervor, closest to its origins, the "I believe" is affirmed in a movement (I believe *in*) that is above all a being-towards. To the relational expressions correspond, at the final stage of movement, so many specifications that particularize its functions. We speak here of relative attributes. But if we allow that every relation presupposes a foundation, we will associate with each of these references an appropriate perfection which, in virtue of the connection of being (*être*) and action (*agir*), opens up to ontological determination.

And in a second moment, under the pressure of circumstances, the ecclesiastical body, threatened with danger from the outside and turbulence from within, emphasizes strong boundaries and the indispensable coherence of a common language. It is the golden age of confessions of faith and dogmatic definitions. The initial movement gains in precision what it loses in élan. The "I believe in . . ." becomes "I believe that. . . ." The collective conscience closes in around a private property or a substance that the magisterium guards as a deposit. The appellations are more controlled. The divine names reflect the certitudes of a tranquil possession.

In a third stage, the very operator of the modality "I believe that" tends be effaced. An exigency of knowledge incites the hope for a rigorous discipline. To the confession of faith, despite its continuation, is substituted the austerity of indicative propositions. God is the object of a science that does not end with examining, in its premises and conclusions, the riches of an empire. It is the age of summas and cathedrals, of theologies of glory in which the Cross seems to have buried itself in triumph for the sake of the "I am that what is" of a well-rested plenitude.

2. This shortcut through history, if its boldness may be forgiven, shows well that faith is never plunged in the unutterable. It is therefore clear that it must speak and name. In this respect, it is thus true that there is a "religious discourse" about a "religious Object." But the problem is less one of knowing if we can or cannot make use of divine names, than it is of appreciating the import we accord them. The names familiar to us, already present in our Scriptures, are less timeless than they seem. They let God be known only by way of our own proper becoming. Even when they function in a "proposition in itself," freed in the saying from any subjective or temporal connotation, the offshore wind draws them back into the boat's wake. And that is why they are always retrospective. They express less "what is" than the history of our attitudes and the passage of God through our individual and social life.

Moreover, to the extent that we are distanced from the origin and from the Cross, ontology becomes heavier, as if the discretion of the beginning, in its relative emptiness, announced a future superabundance. Renewals and reforms have always lived on this contrast between the modesty of the beginning and sumptuousness of the end. At origins, the "divine attributes" (father, spouse, son, and so on) were related to what logicians call "relative individual descriptions." They express relations and functions rather than the determinations of a transcendent *en-soi*. Later, "function" is converted into "substance" or essence by an ever more extensive transposition of determinations of the "here" into constituents of the beyond. These inevitable shifts need not surprise us. Faith is not exempt from this law. It must indeed trace the shadow of our behaviors and discourse upon the interval that separates us from the Principle. Otherwise it would be condemned to nonexistence. But that first movement, of immanence and insertion, must be accompanied by the complementary movement of a second and reflective judgment that puts at a distance the indispensable determinations of our reaching out. In this way the Cross becomes for faith the equivalent of a critical function which, in situating the image in its true place, converts the work of necessity into freedom.

3. That twofold movement of inscription and emergence corresponds to the two fundamental aspects of immersion and detachment signified by the evangelical expression "to be in the world but not of the world." Paul echoes there the "as if" on which Bultmann comments. The first moment, of objectification, puts in play the *dunamis* or fecundity of the Cross. The second should remind us of the fragility and, if one likes, the vanity of all that we do. The one and the other, in their dissoluble unity, are two streams of the same existence, two faces of the same freedom. Has not this Christian freedom, so often a New Testament concern, been put on the back burner or between parentheses? Invention was too long submitted to the "reproduction" of an established order. But a freedom of simple execution or compulsive repetition would be only a caricature. "To obey the Cross" is first to be attuned to it, not to receive assignments but to let ourselves be carried by the offshore wind that will lead we know not where.

For nothing is written on the Sign of the Cross, if not the need to go to the end of the night and of one's very self. The opposition between grace and the law signifies not anarchy but the availability of the spirit of love that drives out the fear and heaviness of the commandments. Nor does it imply the rejection of the past on which "substance" was carried to us. But the necessary is never the sufficient. And it does not suffice to open the master's book to find the answer to our questions. The unceasing rupture established by the Cross is quickly covered over with the weight of our customs. Fear of imagination has obstinately sought the reassuring idea of our predestination in the heavens of fixed stars. Terror of moving sands has hardened into rock the soil of our ground. Thus by turning our back upon the Cross we have changed it into a marble statue. The Nothing par excellence has become the well-established, the *ousia* exploited and consolidated by the labor of centuries. What the Cross demands of us today is a conversion that opens us unconditionally to its hold, without guarantee of security.

Are we then abandoned to the reign of pure indetermination? In this question we suspect a request for readymade solutions, or at least a formula for good and right action. But the Sign contains no germ of an answer that might be explicated through a more or less subtle interpretation. Lacking content, it traces for us lines of orientation. The logic of the Cross would be incomplete if it were limited to a syntax of the Pauline triad or a semantics of the divine names. It must end in a "pragmatics" that throws light upon our action.

IV. FAITH AND CREATION

The tasks of faith in the present world may discourage the fainthearted. Those who are most lucid desire to see clearly in a field of possibilities that demands more than an itemized list. It would not be rash, it seems, to satisfy them in what is most essential. The great axes of our action are drawn in filigree in the key words articulated by the initial paradox: *Logos, Folly, Power.* I will comment freely on their respective thematic value.

1. As to the Logos by which we are both drawn and interrogated, the danger that threatens us, and it is no illusion, can be summed up as the awareness of a sort of exhaustion. Tacitly, we entrust our predecessors with the glory of having already said everything, in order to leave to "the others," ourselves not among them, the prestige of invention. We vacillate between the need for a repetition that spares us from the innovator's pride, and the responsibility for a new Word that would crush our remaining forces. Such is indeed the scandal. The *ex nihilo* of the Cross no longer invites us to creation. Would the question that it puts before us, and that puts a question to us, then be answered forever? Would such an abdication not be very negation of faith, which can never, on pain of idolatry and cowardice, be satisfied with the forms of our past, however beautiful?

Would the past examined by the theologians no longer teach us the mortifying imperative of continual passage? The Cross, I realize, takes us away from our permanent dwelling places. But it does so to invite us to that feast of Tabernacles, of straw or branches, where for a day the Son of Man rests his head.

Our discourse, no doubt, is destined to be ephemeral. We must rejoice in that. The risk of contingency is the only possible response to the call of the one thing necessary. Without wishing to make a "to-do" list for future, the task of a theology would seem to me to be, above all, a "staurology," concerned from now on with a small number of questions:

- Toward where, toward what "region of dissimilitude," is the Sign of Contradiction deporting us?
- To what thought does this singular Sign give rise in the new space in which we are invited to dwell?
- As judgment on the world, what major forms would this judgment take?
- What is the relation between an authentic freedom and the Nothingness or *ex nihilo* of the Christian beginning?
- Of what past do we dispose to support our élan?

I do not presume to fix a closed number of questions. I dwell on the most urgent ones, which concern our dwelling place, our way of inhabiting it, and the power it gives us in respect to the world, which we must transform without becoming its prisoners. These questions are resolved neither by the certainties of dogmatics, nor the erudition of the best informed exegesis, nor the wise positivity of a church history under less surveillance than it used to be. They are only prolegomena, which could easily be arranged into a comprehensive problematic. No discipline, however precious, can exempt us from them.

2. Yet however helpful these questions may be in renewing a rather tired understanding from the perspective of the Cross, I do not forget the aspect of the Sign that engages us within the thickness of everyday life. If the Cross, in its way, is power of God, our practice ought to show its efficacy. Generous intuitions, whose practical value we admit, would be scattered into incoherence if they rejected certain lines of reflection as superfluous.

- What is the relation of the Cross to human pain, work, and suffering?
- What light does it throw on the brutality of death, whose insignificance is promised us in a society that would put and end to its most glaring inequalities?
- How do we understand the exemplariness of the service of which it offers the paradigm?
- What importance does the idea of "salvation" take on today?
- What precise links can be discovered between salvation and justice?

These are burning questions, raised by legitimate concern that we do away with our compromises and indifference. Some may judge them inopportune or demobilizing. Some would secretly reduce them to the nothingness of pseudo-questions. Yet the imperative of lucidity, even of personal integrity, exacts, in every hypothesis, that we know what we do when we claim filiation with the Cross and Resurrection.

3. There remains a last domain, the most foreign and set apart, since it concerns folly, a singular folly in this kingdom blessed with singularities. What do we "make" today of the "folly of the cross"? We can no longer repeat the exploits of former times. Even in forcing ourselves, we would not attain the expected effect. For all that, must we condemn this essential and invincible element to the prudent silence that discreetly cloaks the aberrations of another age? The distinction proposed above, between a stigmatizing participation and the free distance of judgment, suggests less an anachronistic repetition than a perhaps more fruitful and stimulating orientation for a more youthful fantasy.

I will first give expression, for the sake of discussion, to some eccentric questions:

- What relations might we glimpse, near or far, between the "folly of the Cross" and ecstasy, folly, eccentricity?
- More precisely, what value do we accord to the idea of the center, which has for so long dominated speculation?
- In what sense does the divine folly harbor a possibility of dramatization?
- Supposing that this dramatization were necessary, how would it be actualized today?

- More concretely, how can a theater of the Cross be conceived, along the two axes of participation and distance?

Apart from the transpositions that some yet-to-be-born art might effect, the "folly of the Cross"—which is reserved to no specialization or competency—should have an irreplaceable function in the life of faith. What function? In its macroscopic form, it would perhaps be assimilated into the *danse macabre* of the mad god who destroys, in a supreme joy, his own cre- ations, or into the serenity of a sovereign indifference where the light of day and the darkness of night are balanced and counter- balanced. Yet to resolve the folly of the Cross by an appeal to the judgment of equinox would be to misunderstand it. For it is not a question of annihilating what has been made and inscribed in the density of a past, but of establishing in us a more difficult freedom that does not let itself be fascinated with the traces of its passage. Judgment, if you wish, whose true name would be that of religious conversion: the return to the null and sublime point where we dwell and where, when we return to it in the austerity of dispossession, we find again the innocence of a first morning. This vesperal light, dispensed by the folly of the Cross in the third hour, does more than confirm the necessity of a rhythm or the support of an élan, *arsis* and *thesis* reciprocally confirming and supporting one another. Above all, it shows us in the moving baptismal symbolism of participation in the death and Resurrection of Christ, an unsuspecting depth of faith. The medieval mystic knew how to speak of a "seed of non-being" (*germen nihili*) consubstantial with the soul, where, as Meister Eckhart expresses it, "God becomes verdant in all the honor of his being." Can not this strange phrase, echoing a Neoplatonic expression recovered by J. Trouillard (cf. *L'Un et l'Ame selon Proclos*, Paris, 1972, p. 138 s.v.) but no doubt derived from a more ancient tradition, speak to us the last word on the essence of faith through the image of folly? The phrase not only trans- gresses the predicative regime of dogmatic propositions and the ecclesiastical reference of confessional beliefs. It equally ex- ceeds the psychological élan and theological dynamism of an absolute confidence. Truly, at this summit—which has been called "flower of the soul," "flower of fire," "flash of lightening," "star"—faith no longer has an object. Intentional distance is effaced, because, in that supreme nakedness, the concepts of object, distinction, and identity lose all jurisdiction. "Seed of non-being," faith becomes, then, connatural with the god of folly in which it reposes in an acquiescence that raises it above the world and the splendors of ontology. Would this then be the "desert" of the old anchorites? The desert would be rather the "locative" image of that "non-being," which is the promise of a universe. *Toda y nada:* "being nothing, the soul can become everything." But this world that it must create will always be that theater which demands at once the solemnity of a creation and *also* the sweet irony that regards from afar, in a darkness of a "sorrow without cause," the human and divine comedy in which people and things play out their game of chance, necessity, and sorrow.

The logic of the Cross, taken in its entirety, thus comports many dimensions. It is not content with establishing, in the staurological triad, a connection between Logos and Power by the middle term of Folly. This first conclusion provokes a new reflection on the paradox of the Nothing, which calls into question the validity of our attributions, determined, in the Pauline perspective, by the prestige of power and wisdom. Certainly, denominations are necessary, and it is not a question of contesting them. What is essential is that we not be victims of our necessities. The "divine names" indeed express something; but what they express loses every constitutive or determinant character of a transcendent fullness. Heretofore, we must hear them more dynamically, as traces or images of an evolution of faith which, in the course of its history, arrays the unclothed god whose message it proclaims with the always limited and sometimes compromising excellences inspired by a "service of the Cross, more or less well understood." In this sense, every semantics reflects the vicissitudes of time, the tendencies of an epoch, the élans and the burdens of the individual or the community. Its value is measured, in the final analysis, by the realizations that it sums up, because the being of the new god is in some way at the mercy of the faithful. It is what we will be, in response to a prevenient grace that imposes neither exemplariness nor predestination. To faith, then, returns the stirring and formidable mission of inscribing, in its forms and transfigurations, the power of the Cross.

6

The Enigma of Kenosis

THE HYMN from the Epistle to the Philippians (2, 5–11) cannot be dissociated from the other Pauline text that has guided us thus far. The two pericopes respond to and complete one another. The first accents folly, the second infirmity. The one stresses the Logos of the new kerygma and its characteristics; the other, the practice of faith that it motivates by the example of Christ:

> Who, subsisting in the form of God
> did not count equality with God
> something to be grasped.
> But he emptied himself,
> taking the form of a slave,
> becoming as human beings are;
>> and being in every way like a human being
> he was humbler yet,
> even to accepting death,
>> death on a cross.
>
> And for this God raised him high,
> and gave him the name
> which is above all other names;
>
> so that *all beings*
> in the heavens, on earth
>> and in the underworld,
>> *should bend the knee* at the name of Jesus
>> and that every *tongue should acknowledge*
>> Jesus Christ as Lord,
>> To the glory of God the Father. (Jerusalem Bible)

I. DIVINE FORM, SLAVE FORM

1. However uncertain specific points of translation may be, the structure of the passage is clear enough to rule out any hesita-

tion about its overall meaning. The movement of the whole is
ordered by a threefold rhythm that, recalling our school days,
we would be tempted to translate by a law of three states. It
indeed concerns a movement, for in parsing it, the breaks that
seem to interrupt are not stases from which to recompose it.
The repose of subsisting in which Christ dwells is already ani-
mated by a concern. It opens up the possibility of a procession
that follows, in an intentional progression, the descent of the
divine into a human form, obedience unto death, the ignominy
of the Cross. But at the very moment that the paroxysm of
abasement touches the depth of nothingness, the shock of the
negative, in its paradoxical power, commands the exultant ascent toward the point of origin.

Abstracting its contents, a superficial reading recognizes, in
this formal arrangement, a classical schema of intelligibility
used in its threefold rhythm by a great many philosophies and
theologies. At least, we sense here the outline of certain more
scholarly dialectics: the *en-soi* of subsisting, traversed by an im-
perceptible line, is inverted in an exodus of exteriorization and
alienation at exhaustion, to rejoin the sublime beginning, at the
end of exhaustion, in a glorious and victorious return.

2. This order we have discerned, underscored by the key
words "subsisting," "emptying," and "elevation," consists of
some more concrete elements that the letter itself asks us not
to forget. The kenotic exodus sketches out a hierarchical condescension in which the form of the slave passes through distinct
and interdependent degrees of humanity, death, and the Cross.
In similarly sequential stages, but in inverted order, the return
proceeds: the name above every name heals the unspeakable
infamy of the crucified; resurrection conquers death; the divine
Lordship transforms the human and servile form.

Yet this excess of fullness, which crowns kenosis, is not a simple return that would do nothing more than restore the initial
state. Something has really happened that cannot be effaced or
assimilated into the pure negation of the negation. The event
concludes with the advent of a new Reign. It must be admitted,
then, that the kenotic process introduces into the divine sphere
a certain becoming. We will try to dissolve this enigma. In its

totality, this becoming, if we explicate its internal logic, suggests the fivefold transformation of the original schema:

(a) subsistence in form of God (*auprès de*)
(b) assumption of the human form
(c) obedience of the servant unto the death of the cross
(d) exaltation above all the powers (of heaven, of earth, of the underworld)
(e) glory of the name above every name

Between the two extremes of subsistence and glory, obedience unto death represents the mediating center. But this median itself presupposes, as condition of possibility, the mediation of human form, which stands between the divine subsistence and submission. Symmetrically, between obedience and the glory of the name, the exaltation above the powers inserts a new middle term that relates within it the contrasting polarities. The sequence traced by this genesis entails a "relation of motivation" that binds the elements of the series more closely together.

3. This exposition has been only an introduction to the problems posed by a disconcerting text whose metaphysical resonances hardly seem to fit its context of exhortation and edification. By its terminology, as by its general appearance, it elicits questions beyond the competencies of the pure exegete. In a study that seemed exhaustive in its day, Paul Henry offered a detailed but clear summary of interpretations given this text by the Greek and Latin Fathers as well as by Protestant and Orthodox theologians from the sixteenth century onward (see "Kénose," in *Supplément du dictionnaire du Bible*). Henry's study contains a considerable summary of information on both possible or probable Jewish or pagan sources of the text, as well as traditional and innovative interpretations that have attempted to resolve its difficulties. I will not try to add to it. I prefer, in a first stage, to reflect on this long history. Then, making use of another vein, unrecognized till now by Christian theologians and opened up for us by the erudite studies of Henry Corbin, I will consider certain thought-provoking directions of Muslim mysticism. These preliminaries will help me, in union with what

has gone before, to formulate the theory that I propose about the folly of the Cross.

II. INTERPRETATIONS

1. The patristic interpretation, on the whole and in its speculative continuation by Catholic theologians, proposes in principle that all possibly correct understandings of kenosis must be submitted to the major axiom of divine immutability. It thus excludes any evidence that would alter ever so slightly the purity of the Absolute in its richness and simplicity. The light of the *Esse Subsistens* tolerates no shadow of change. As regards any question of essence, attributes, or Trinitarian processions, the very thought of a change, even under the specious motivation of an intense love, has the blasphemous savor of an insult or the naivete of reckless anthropomorphism. The divine condescension in no way affects the being of God, and the "giving" referred to in Scripture allows for no contamination, however subtle, that would accommodate it to the destiny of the human psyche. Certain thinkers, of Catholic inspiration, have attempted to welcome suffering in God, sublimating "suffering" by raising it to the dignity of a "simple perfection." Citing a text that advises not "saddening the Spirit of God," they have thought, for example, that a certain sadness that flowered discreetly among us in the saints might not be unworthy of the Most High. I willingly recognize that in another cultural context the idea of a "divine sadness" gave rise to a very original mysticism. But in respect to the authors in question and their Christian perspective, we must admit the difficulty of adapting to the Elysian serenity of the All-Powerful a "passion" whose depressive and diminutive character seems to forbid every exaltation into what are properly called attributes. Although psychosociological or philosophical reasons may suggest emotion in "The One Who Is," it remains clear that this theological promotion implies no concession to kenosis properly understood, for far from impoverishing it, it adds one more flower to the solitary crown of the Most Real Being. For, in the most constant tradi-

tion of Catholic thought, annihilation takes place exclusively in the creature, that is, in the human nature of Christ. No doubt, the assumption of the human within the unity of a same person authorizes, by the very tenor of the dogma, the "communication of idioms," the logical exchange of properties. But according to classical theology, the unity of the center of attribution in no way legitimizes the confusion of essences or domains. According to the doctrine, so often recalled and translated by the theology of "mixed relations," "God touches without being touched." Real from our side, the relation can only be "reasonable" when we transform it into its converse. Thus the theology of kenosis remains completely faithful to the rigors of an onto-theology, that is, of a metaphysics of being as being which, in its eminence and eternal immobility contains the infinite totality of infinite perfections.

2. In the larger circle of Christian theologies that are not Catholic, the God of faith enjoys the advantage of a coefficient of elasticity, if you will forgive the expression, that varies considerably according to understandings. I cannot enter into the maze of explanations—distinctions between relative attributes (such as all-powerful) and absolute attributes constituting the divine nature, between possession and usage—without counting the subtleties of the procession of the Word who suffers an eclipse at the moment of incarnation. We are sometimes irritated with this self-mutilating god, who sometimes loses what he has and sometimes regains what he has lost. But this unfortunate impression is corrected as soon as we realize what is really in play beneath these disconcerting moves. The kenotic solutions, of course, respond to specifically Christian problems, imposed by the dogmas of councils concerned more specifically with the union in the man Jesus of the human and divine. Yet beneath these regional problems lies the more fundamental question of the union between the finite and the infinite. To resolve this aporia, these multiple responses were created, which basically face the same difficulty: how can the divinity be truly united with the humanity, if, immutable in its self-sufficiency, it persists, so to speak, in its absoluteness? It seems that if the relation is to be more than simply external, such as

that of worker to product, the Supreme must proceed, by a spontaneous renunciation, to a condescension that humbles its ontological level and creates within it the need or void that the world and the human would fulfill. An old scholastic axiom specifies that two substances, active and full, are susceptible only to an accidental union or a joining of simple juxtaposition. The two extremes must therefore take form as "empty power and act" to give rise to an authentic unity. That is why an immemorial tradition, echoed in certain philosophies, postulates as the world's condition of possibility a restriction of being that gives place, in God, to what is not God. We will translate this postulate roughly in the following way: if God is the all of being, how could God be other than God's own self? Truly, God would be isolated by this omni-perfection within an egoistic transcendence that would detract from the most beautiful divine attribute, Love: Love that cannot be conceived without suffering and abnegation. Moreover, if we consider the Christian doctrine of the Logos as the pleroma of exemplary ideas in which "all that has been was life in God," does it not make sense to assert that the creature itself, in its ideal existence, is absolutely indispensable to the divine being? The unity of the finite and the infinite, in this perspective, overflows the supposedly contingent fact of the world's existence. The absolute and the relative are already reciprocally necessary to one another from all eternity, as being to the being and the being to being. And if one objects that the God of faith is degraded by being destined thus to loss, it is replied that the unconditional surrender of the Christian God to the metaphysics of being risks, as Paul feared, emptying the Cross of Christ, essential component of the Object of faith. Change and imperfection, we might add, have been too often confounded. And above all, an unremovable *par soi* has been identified with a questionable *pour soi* that imprisons the divinity within the systematic enclosure of aseity. According to a well-known definition, matter is "the fixed will of a fixed state." If we reject such a materialism, and if, moreover, we admit in God an effective will, it seems impossible not to introduce an element of mobility that cannot be dissociated from our idea of freedom.

This freedom, for our theologians, would not be flexible in every sense. Not only is God not free to be unfree, but God cannot choose between an "absolute goodness" and a diabolical perversity, as certain philosophies have imagined. God is love; freedom and love coincide in God. And that is why God is capable of a change whose true name would be "sacrifice." Kenosis is similar to sacrifice; the Cross and kenosis are at the very heart of God, in that eternal sacrifice in which God is priest and victim. The Pauline hymn says nothing else. It exhorts us to a new understanding of the depths of God.

3. The interpretation of these theological theses, which were not accessible to me in the original, will no doubt seem to the better-informed to be too obviously driven by philosophic references. I am not sure. But if its pertinence is admitted, it makes sense to advance the reflection it nourishes. A second reading allows a twofold judgment.

First, the reaction of surprise at these strange histories that scandalize the common sense of the faithful is tempered when we recall the classical mythologies, which are also fond of divine metamorphoses. When we plunge back into the élan of the kenotic hymn, the difference is the distinction between an actively flowering imagination and the gravity of a dramatization that plays out to its logical end the seriousness of divine love.

Yet the most fruitful lesson is not this recollection of antiquity, but a connection with an entirely different import. In fact, the insistence, common to these theologies, on the free will that dominates from on high the divine being and having, evokes the formula of Plotinus according to which the One makes itself what it wants to be, as "cause of itself." But the boldness of the expression, which liberates from the ineffable the most beautiful of its human names, is immediately qualified in their philosophy by an "as if" whose prudence has been lost in the Christian exegesis of kenosis. Among the more intrepid of our interpreters, the prestige of the essence remains uncontaminated, since the God of sacrifice transcends and respects necessity. In contrast, Neoplatonism radicalizes the Platonic "beyond being."

Perhaps, and this is only a fragile hypothesis, we have been interpreting too literally these striking texts, whose real power consists less in their immediate meaning than in their power to disconcert. The kenotic dramaturgy seems to describe the events of a self-emptying that hesitates, in a certain sense, before its ultimate consequences. If our suggestion is accepted, the final intention of this sublime theater, by emphasizing a will to love that would renounce all possession, signifies the need to transcend the conceptual schemas of an ontology that has heavily strained the historical representations of faith. The transposition, to the Christian God, of the "causality of the self by the self," by the mediation of pure love, evokes less the heroic epic of a theogenesis than the torment of a magnificent *Agape* concerned with giving itself without condition or restriction. This moving image of sacrifice and emptying unfolds schematically to make us aware of the emergence of a sovereign freedom, whose ecstasy of giving requires as preamble the rejection of every richness, of substance or attributes.

A more detailed examination of the works surveyed might contradict this hesitantly advanced exegesis. If proven plausible, it would give valuable confirmation to our interpretation of the folly of the Cross. The two approaches, however, do not recover one another. I will clarify, in what follows, the impact of the kenotic hymn on a theology of the Cross. Meanwhile, I will give the previously mentioned detour, by way of Islam, the attention it deserves for opening a new horizon for ecumenical meditation.

III. The "Divine Sadness" in Sufism

For this voyage into unknown lands I will cite Henry Corbin's *The Creative Imagination in the Sufism of Ibn Arabi* (1976). I will retain some themes related to the question we have raised.

1. This mysticism speaks to us, indeed, of a "divine sadness" that would be the origin of the world. What is it really about? Condensing our research as much as possible, we can say that this apparent defect in the "diamond of the Absolute" is the function of its very transcendence. For God is beyond all knowl-

edge, every concept. His being and essence lie hidden in a density of night that out of excess and according to an immemorial dialectic calls out to the light. "The divine being aspires to be revealed in all things." It aspires to be named. More exactly, the divine names that proliferate in a "cloud of unknowing" themselves suffer from an infinite sadness. They also aspire, and in an unspeakable anguish, to be named. In a "sigh of compassion," the divine sadness empathizes with their anguish, repeating itself from sorrow to sorrow, which has nothing to do with a "thought of the thought." And it is this sigh that awakens it to the possibility of their actualization. But they and their respective attributes can be named only by concrete subjects whose individual form responds to their expectation and aspiration.

2. A reciprocal exchange is established between the divine names and the human subjects determined by them. If the divine names give rise to those who name them, inversely those who name them give existence to their creator. Each individual is in this way suspended by a name that determines its existence. But since active and passive are distributed on two levels, each one is responsible for the being of God in its theophany. The relation between the divine name and its human epiphany is not, therefore, what Christian dogmas designate by the expression "hypostatic union." It is a relation between a sovereign or lord and servant. This service is a slavery of love, resembling only slightly the courtly love of the Middle Ages. It is active love, for "if the divine name creates my being, my being establishes it reciprocally in the very act through which it establishes me" (Corbin, p. 234, note 33). This is the common and mutual passion that Corbin names *unio sympathica,* or sympathetic union, highlighting its opposition to hypostatic union. The primordial love of "compassion" by which God desires to be revealed, giving rise to its revelations and revealers, becomes in us "the compassionate love" that moves us to show it forth. We find here the stunning anticipation of the formulas of Spinoza and Hegel; according to these, the love by which we love God is identical with the love by which he loves himself and knows himself in revealing himself in us. A corollary in the *Ethics* (V, proposition 36) indeed specifies: "God, in so far as he loves

himself, loves humankind and, in consequence, the love of God for humankind and the intellectual love of the soul for God are one and the same thing." As Bergson will later say, where we see two movements there is really only one. But we must add that the infinite sadness, which coincides with the original love, is, in the final analysis, the breath, the spirit, the immaterial and angelic substance "from which all beings are formed."

3. In focusing on the subject, I have doubtlessly overlooked the most beautiful of these roses of Isaphan whose colors and perfumes the author has so generously dispensed. To conclude this useful digression, I would like to make clear the reasons for its inadequacy.

What makes this path fascinating is the fact that in the Christian context, as on Islamic earth, it is a question of a god of pathos who leaves his solitude, who becomes human in a servant related to his lord by a reciprocal love of service. We are seduced by this "ellipse of which one foyer is the being of God for and by me, and the second my being by and for him, since my knowledge of him is his knowledge of me"(ibid., p. 144). At the origin, we specify, there is "not an autocratic omnipotence but a fundamental nostalgia, the sadness of a solitude, and such is the motive that makes the absolute being a creator: sadness is the secret of creativity" (ibid.).

Yet this creativity has nothing to do with a production *ad extra,* because "it is impossible to conceive of being exterior to the absolute being." Theophany is thus substituted for the Judeo-Christian creation. It dispenses us from a blasphemous and impossible hypostatic incarnation, since "God is not me and I am not God: simply, he is epiphanized in me" (ibid., p. 240). These differences are serious, even though we can discuss their validity on certain points. They do not directly concern the Pauline text.

I underscore a final trait of similarity: the descent of God into the human form of the servant who reveals him is correlative to the ascension and exaltation of the servant in the glory of God he makes exist. The going forth is simultaneously a return, since real unity, this side of confusion and separation, permits two different perspectives on the same movement. We can then dis-

cern in the diverse languages of going forth and return an analogy of structure in which there are elements and functions in
each that truly seem to correspond to one another. It is precisely
this suspicion of a hidden similarity that even today can lead
the philosopher or Christian theologian into the temptation of a
sympathetic voyage.

4. A more exacting reflection risks dissipating this impression
of cordial accord. A necessarily partial summary seems to ne-
glect, by generosity or abstraction, the "contextual sense" that
gives the words of the lexicon their bouquet of terror. The God
of the Cross, in spite of appearances, is not and cannot be that
of the Sufi mystic. Since the first discourages all ontological attributions, the transcendence of the second, even veiled with
the darkness of the unknowable, enjoys an essence whose all-
comprehensive richness is distributed in the infinity of names
and perfections that qualify his eminence. Therefore the journey we have attempted, from "infinite sadness" to kenosis, slips
into the equivocation of a false reconnaissance. Why? If we remember that the divine sadness or "compassion" from which all
beings would be molded is at once the love of God for himself
and the aspiration toward his own manifestation, we recognize
the distance that separates such a love from a kenotic love,
which cannot be even obliquely concerned for itself and its revelation. To avoid unfairness, I take care not to minimize the
admirable teaching according to which "the love by which God
loves himself is identical to the love by which we love him." But
if God truly loves himself and knows himself "in us, by us," it
no less remains that, in the order of reasons, it is because he
first loves himself, even through the veil of infinite sadness, that
he can love himself in us and by us. This second love moves,
necessarily, in the circle of ipseity traced around it by infinite
sadness, as infinite need of a space in which the divine fullness
unfolds itself in order to affirm itself. Sadness here seems, indeed, to reinforce the impossibility of self-forgetting. Spinoza,
whose future presence is anticipated by the Sufi formulas,
speaks also of the love by which God loves himself. But it is a
question there, in his terminology, only of a mode, of an infinite
mode and not of an actual attribute. The "intellectual love of

God," while always in the divine circle of influence, takes place only in the sphere of the *nature naturée*. Similarities will therefore be corrected "by a greater dissimilarity." As for *Agape*, it cannot be referred, in the optic of the Cross, to the subject that inspires it. To repeat a celebrated distinction, it is of the "ecstatic" and no longer of the "physical" order. That is what is implied by the kenosis, which we must discuss again in what remains.

Finally I point to a last differentiating trait in the mysticism of Ibn Arabi. It is not only that "God is a beautiful being" but "beauty itself," attribute par excellence, whose spiritual and creative power "creates love in humankind, invites imagination and awakens nostalgia for the beyond." That is why the feminine, "which is neither temptation nor fall," has such importance in this doctrine; not only because "the terms which mark the origin, cause and divine essence are (grammatically) feminine," but because feminine beauty represents, for the mystic and for the "servant of the divine Lord," the "metaxu" or indispensable mediation that collects, in a canticle of canticles, the universal epiphany of the divinity. The *doulos* of the Epistle to the Philippians knows no such marvelous attraction. He is exhausted and dispersed in the unconditional service of those whom he has come to serve. It is not a question, let us note, of multiplying these divergences, of pronouncing a judgment or assigning prizes for excellence, but of loyally marking a distinction that no artifice can efface. It is good for the different to differ to the maximum, and for the diverse, in the universe where they meet without being confounded, to be desired for itself without some notion of hierarchy lurking in the background.

This journey on foreign soil will not, then, have been useless if it permits us to better discern what the kenotic hymn says. It remains for us to discover, as best we can, the essential meaning that we were tempted to misunderstand.

IV. KENOSIS AND THE CROSS

1. It must first be recalled that the hymn unfolds in a context of exhortation, which excludes or at least renders improbable a

metaphysical sort of interpretation. The Philippians are concerned above all with changing their spirits and hearts by modeling them on the example of Christ Jesus.

Since this *metanoia* touches at once the mind and heart, the transformation evoked by kenosis concerns, simultaneously, the image we form of God and Christ and the conduct inspired by it. What, then, is this image, which is cut out, like all images, from the social fabric it reflects? The text suggests it irresistibly to us. It is that of the ruler who reproduces "the form of God" in its most striking traits, in its supremacy of power and perfection. This image, we insist, is not the work of an individual fantasy, which would stage the spectacle of its productions in a gratuitous game. In a certain way, it is imposed by the conditions of the milieu. And that is why, far from being arbitrary, it responds, as we have said, to a "necessary mode of conceptualizing." This necessity explains its relative universality, its obvious extension. What changed with the Cross is precisely that ruling image. Heretofore, the role of kenosis is to call it into question, not by a scholarly contestation but by the sole power of another image that is admirably suited to the sign of the Cross.

2. Orthodox theologians had reason to reject any alteration of the god of their cherished tradition that would have modified, in its essence or contours, the being of the Absolute. They maintained a coherent image that was not that of the new god. Bolder theologians, who understandably read into the Pauline text the course of a reversal, made just one error: they did not radicalize their interrogation of a certain ontology. Both the Orthodox theologians and their bolder counterparts moved, in the final analysis, on the same terrain. From the outset it was necessary to move to another place, and be situated without reluctance at that null point of the Cross where, in the distance taken, the idols simultaneously confirm and lose the solidity of their configuration.

3. In this empty heaven, another image takes its relief, the image at the center of the hymn, which raises the figure of the *doulos* to the dignity of an absolute. We usually translate this Greek term as "servant," doubtlessly because the "servant of

Yahweh," one of the probable sources of our text, is imposed on the horizon of the reader. But perhaps we should not insist as much on an historical precedent, however thoroughly detailed, as on the quasi-sculptural "form" of the slave, that singular essence whose being consists precisely in not being. In his commentary on John 15, 15 s.v., St. Thomas appears to me to have defined succinctly, making use of prepositions, this condition of the *doulos*.

> Properly speaking, the slave is someone who is not cause of himself. There is, therefore, a difference between the operations of the slave and those of the free person. For the slave acts in the sight and cause of another, while the free being operates by reason of itself and according to the final cause and motive cause: in effect, the free being acts for itself as being its own end, and acts by itself because it puts itself to work on the sole motive of its will. But the slave acts neither for himself, because he works for another, nor by himself, because he is moved and constrained by a foreign will.

Here the theologian's brevity rejoins the austerity of a limit concept. We must underscore the decisive words—cause of self, by self, for self—as their symmetric negatives. In light of this philosophical explanation, what gives rise to thought in the link between the "form of God" and the "form of the slave" is that those otherwise noble ideas that we associate with the affirmation of God (among others and above all that of the self cause, and the harmonies with which it enriches the ancient notion of substance while deepening it) are no longer in play from this point on. The space in which the message must be understood has nothing to do with that in which we find ourselves, whether spontaneously or by inertia. Ultimately, the very idea of a divine Self becomes null and void. The conversion demanded at the level of an intelligence of faith thus rejoins the transformation invited by the staurological verses of the First Epistle to the Corinthians. Yet, although Paul once overthrew the names of an ontological theology that partially joined, at a common intersection, the two Jewish and Greek currents of a religious Mediterranean, the kenotic hymn, whose authorship matters little, attacks the very root of these attributions. The Sign of contra-diction accomplishes its "méontology" in the form of the slave in which every memory of the I or the self dies. The two mo-ments of the Cross are joined in a reciprocal passage which, on the one hand, suppresses the divine excellences in the ruin of their foundation and, on the other, inversely, dissipates the fun-damental ipseity in the annulment of its infinite riches. In this way is opened up the possibility of a new consciousness or a new horizon that will be the new earth or the new heaven of faith.

4. Therefore kenosis will no longer be what it had to be along the lines we have inventoried. The more traditional theology minimized its impact in order to reduce it to an extrinsic de-nomination. The dramaturgical theologies of the East or West overestimated the effects of some ascetical dispossession within the Absolute itself.

Both sides misunderstood the true "becoming." In reality, the process is accomplished integrally at the interior of the soul which, in the austerity without complacency of this purgative way, purifies itself of those superabundant litanies with which it once favored its God. In ridding itself of the splendors with which it gifted the Most High, it operates a reduction that con-figures it to the "form of a slave," in order to realize its power. Shall we say that it loses or gains by this dispossession of itself? Loss and gain bring us back too often to economic considera-tions. Perhaps, to avoid prosaic terms and adopt a language that is not without pitfalls, we might better say that the soul, at the end of its way of the cross, recovers that native nudity described in diverse ways by an ancient tradition in the formula "the soul has no nature if not that of having none." In reading upon the Cross and on the "form of the slave" the desert-like severity of the new god, it returns to its proper depths. The nakedness of the soul responds to the nakedness of its god.

Without resolving the problem, it seems to us that the enig-matic union that dogma tried to express as the hypostatic link between two natures, human and divine, shines forth at that empty and sublime point. The profound meaning of the formula is not to be sought along the lines of an Aristotelian ontology,

but rather, inversely, on the side of a "méontology." Indeed, at
that level to which we are lifted up by the Cross, private properties or distinct natures do not matter. The properties, whatever
they be, can only divide what ought to be united. If, at this
summit or at this abyss, exclusive determinations vanish, they
no longer impede unity. Their absence even conditions the most
profound unity.

This seems to us to be the first lesson to be drawn from the
kenotic hymn. Yet we would be lacking in critical spirit if, having
dismissed the pretense of the theology of the ruler, we were to
renew the game of attributions in the opposite direction. I recalled above, on this subject, that contraries, however opposed,
remain in the same genre. The new God is therefore beyond
patron and slave, beyond despotic affirmation and humiliated
negation. But if, to eliminate any sectarianism, we must avoid
correcting an excess by a defect, it nonetheless remains that the
point of the text, in its ultimate message, inclines us to privilege
the language of service. The most up-to-date representations,
those that appeal to our most natural inclinations, glorify positions canonized by the social milieu. In the Christian, the movement of faith proceeds against this inclination and through a
twist that strips us of certain common sense. The figure of the
slave, in such an accused relief, is more than an image that in
an iconoclasm of the imagination shatters the idol of power. Yet
more than a sign for a new understanding of the things of God,
it is a categorical imperative toward life and action.

How is this imperative to be understood? The question is
hardly surprising. The temptation would be to reply to it quickly
in a fine-sounding word that would resolve all the difficulties. I
won't detail the ironies to which the *Agape* has been so often
condemned. But I do recognize that in being made the key that
would unlock every door, it was reduced to the insignificance of
a vague term, as vague as the term "to be," even though that
speaks less to the sensibility. Truly, the heart that affirms itself
in *Agape* is as far from sensible souls as from beautiful souls.
Like the Sufi, it does not distance itself far enough from the
feminine form of beauty. It is, besides, too active to satisfy good
intentions. The Pauline hymn to love knows nothing of the

charms of the Canticle of Canticles and the whiteness of hands that have done nothing. It can only refer to the Cross that liberates, or ought to liberate, the enthusiasm of a creation *ex nihilo*. I say indeed: enthusiasm. Faced with the historical face of the slave, it is indeed impossible to subscribe to the violence that constrains him and condemns him forever to forced labor. The Son of Man retains the form of the slave only to render it insupportable and to make the condition of an incomparable joy surge in the forgetfulness of self: that which raises to the dignity of selfhood the disinherited of every kind, who must be able to say: I am what I am. *Agape* is inseparable from this liberating service, which makes of nothingness not only something but someone. It is then, on this depth of divine and human nothingness, that the substantive "to be" takes the relief that saves it at once from tediousness and pomposity.

And yet, when we have done all this, we must not be satisfied. For if it is true that it is necessary to act for there to be something beyond any principle of sufficient reason, it is forbidden to seek therein the unchanging enjoyment of our face and body, as if fixed in bygone days. We can only go forward, but do so indefinitely. Every return projects the idol's menace upon the past. The resurrection that should be surrection, "using up of," a new world, is not separated from the Cross that detaches us from it. It is not only because faith "is experienced in the movement of going ever forward," and always finds what to do. This restless mobility risks concealing a final ruse that would attach us to a morose pleasure in our own development. The judgment of faith excludes all partiality. It remains faithful to the Cross, which leans toward neither one side nor the other, bringing us back to that empty point from which all that is goes forth in order to return to it. If we should be promised a world in which everything would be virtually accomplished, that totality would betray its own lie and illusion. Servants, we will never acquit ourselves of the debt of service. But the necessity of action also intimates to us the impossibility of establishing our dwelling here. We must choose between this necessary and that impossible. They are the two arms of the Cross. And at the exact point of their crossing resides the joy "that no one will take from you."

7

Johannine Logos, Pauline Logos

IT IS DIFFICULT not to notice the distance and contrast between Paul's presentation of the Logos at the crossroads of
kenosis and folly, and that of John, traditionally so rich in attributes. The question comes immediately to mind: are these two
interpretations of the Word compatible? Supposing that they
exclude one another, how is the faith that admits both not torn
by a division that calls into question its common sense and good
faith?

I will therefore interrogate the modality through which the
Logos is presented in the Johannine Prologue, the differences
that oppose it to the Word of the Cross, and the way in which
faith, through the diversity of these languages, can confront
their proper conflicts.

I. THE WORD OF SPLENDOR

The Johannine Prologue has given rise, as we know, to an impressive number of commentaries, as if the theological and dogmatic tradition has recognized the essentialness of its creed
assembled there on a page. Among the most significant that
were accessible to me, I have retained those of Thomas Aquinas
and Meister Eckhart. But for the sake of contrast, I do not exclude recourse to some more modern studies and contrasting
conclusions, in particular, R. Bultmann's *Das Evangelium des
Johannes* (Gottingen, 1959, pp.1–68). To avoid any ambiguity, I
recall that the Word of splendor to which I refer derives from a
classical exegesis, which in practice had the force of law by the
canonical sanction brought to it by diverse magisterial authorities. This status throws into relief the contrast I am going to
discuss.

1. *The Logos in itself.* In a first reading, however cursory, the text leaves the impression of an entire movement that originates in the Word in "its Principle," unfolds itself in creation, and is achieved in the Incarnation in which a regime of grace and truth is substituted for the Law of Moses. The global movement is marked by the principle caesuras through which it is articulated and around which are organized three textual subsets. As Aquinas observes, the first concerns the Logos in itself; the second is directed at the Word in its productive operation; the third centers upon "that which became flesh." I will characterize them briefly. Speculative exegesis has indeed underscored the prepositional language that specifies the being and condition of the Word. It is, at once, *in, toward,* and *about (auprès de)* God. The order of the particles delineates the ordained ensemble of relations, movements, and operations. "Being-in," in which Thomas recognizes the affirmation of "consubstantiality," designates the null operation of "remaining." "Being-toward" marks a first distance that Thomistic dogma will translate by the theory of constitutive relations distinguishing the divine persons.

"Being-about" operates on the distance, without annulling it, and on a conversion and return that Luke indicates, in his fashion, in the response of Jesus: "Do you not know that I must be about my Father's business?" (2,49–50)

The relational interpretation of this singular condition depends, according to our ancient masters, on a metaphysics of thought and of the "mental Word" produced by it, as well as a conception of sign and image as interior expression of "separating-thinking." The origin is doubtlessly Greek, however original the adaptation. I will synthesize the complexity as follows: Thought, as thought of the thought, that is to say of itself, produces a Logos, at once sign, image, and expression, in and by which it thinks itself as substantial and distinct identity.

We need to retain here not so much the more or less technical detail of the explanations as the unstable equilibrium manifest in them between substance and relation. Bultmann was no doubt right in observing that nothing is said to us about the nature of the Word, but that the accent is placed above all on its functions. In contrast, the theologian of former times, in fidelity to conciliar definitions, had to reconcile identity and distinction. Thus the Word had to inherit, in its very difference, the essence and attributes of the divinity. Difficult conjunction of the "substantial" and the "relative," from which aporias have surged! For us, more sensible to the distinction between a logic of attribution and a logic of relations, the assumed harmony seems to be effaced before an alternative. Either we think of the Word according to the schema of the Most Real Being, of whom can be predicated innumerable perfections, or we opt firmly for function and relation, for that relation said to have "consisted in a passage." The second position, we admit, would be closer to the sign of the Cross, at least if one agrees that, of itself, relation connotes no perfection. Moreover, by evoking a continual "transit," it awakens in us I know not what lightness or self-oblivion which, in an angel's wing, projects against every fixed visage or establishment the joy of passing and of dying.

2. *The Exodus into the World.* The second group of texts defines the transitive operation that manifests the Word in the world, echoing through creation the *fiat lux* of origins. The creative act is introduced at the point where two substantives, *life* and *light,* are joined. More precisely, "the life is the light of humankind," as if the world, as trace of a generous initiative or ebullience, could be "world" only through its recollection in a human thought, in which the Word would be both the thinker and the thought. If, indeed, "everything has been made by Him," humankind must interrogate the whole, rising above its immensity and defiantly detaching itself from it in order to submit it, thus distanced and problematized, to the judgment's freedom. We are reminded here of another evangelical statement: "You are in the world, you are not of the world." But the sole fact of this interrogation mark betrays a rupture which, however servile we have formerly been, permits us to be slaves no longer. Autonomy, however, is not an end in itself. It was given us so that we would recognize in *the fact of what is* the result of a creation, and in this very creation the donatary source that inspired it. All cognition (*connaissance*) is recognition (*reconnaissance*) in the twofold sense of the word.

The vocabulary of life and light, which is frequently used by the evangelist John and is not peculiar to Christianity, received a very special attention by medieval commentators. For Meister Eckhart, life is effervescence, a "bubbling over" that has two currents, so to speak: the internal "overflowing" opens out into the immanent or Trinitarian processions; the external is but the outpouring of those great waters overflowing in the actual creation. But whatever its orientation, this marvelous Zoè is enchanted by superabundance. She has outside of herself neither cause nor end. She is truly "cause of the self" and her beatitude is but the enjoyment of her all-powerful excess.

The light, in contrast, seems to walk on the waves to convert them to wisdom. The Logos-light is the serenity of laws and exemplary ideas. Architectural calculation, whose models obsess the theologian, makes use of means to adjust them to its ends. The world becomes "machine," admirably combined in its game of causes and effects, to render glory to the Creator. But, sometimes, a more poetic note crosses this very rational liturgy. Being, observes Eckhart, "is the word by which God speaks and calls out to all things." Every being is a response to a first Word, a voice, like that of John the Baptist, which cries out in the anonymous desert and animates the very stones to become "children of God" in anticipation.

3. *The Word made flesh.* The light that passes through the shadows and the voice that passes over the stones have always announced the One who was to come. They take a more decisive form in that series of patriarchs and prophets, who, according to the Epistle to the Hebrews, have chanted the stages of a long procession in so many divine words. John the Baptist concludes a lineage and an itinerary. Yet in this final phase, he is only forerunner and witness. He disappears in his mission, as if its élan had devoured his human substance and identity. He still cries out in the desert, as if this excess of emptiness was needed in order that the fullness of time appear at last. With a finger that cannot touch what it indicates, he points to the Lamb of God and light of the world. Until now, indeed, there were only gropings in a night that sketched, in vaguely penciled lines and an incessant combat with the shadows, the visage of the man who would be the face of the Absolute on earth. The Word

made flesh fulfills the imperative of an immemorial last breath: "Come, Lord Jesus." He fills out with his presence the precursor's indicative. In him, by him, and for him, definitive Revelation is realized, since no more profound unity between man and God could be realized without pain of confusion. The theology of the incarnate Word, at least its most striking essentials, thus implies the well-known postulate: "The more and the less, in every order, exist and are articulated only in relation to a maximum." The historical and universal interval that stretches from origins to the final apocalypse is thus explained in a "canticle of degrees," whose stages, in an eternally designed succession, constitute a strictly and totally ordained whole. Jesus Christ recapitulates and consummates the perfections dispersed in the diversity of beings and things. He is the authentic Maximum of whom we have all received. Alpha and Omega of the universal evolution, he is both that by which everything proceeds and that toward which everything that comes to be moves and dies, by orientation and ultimate finality. At this summit, on which are gathered the cosmic excellences of nature and grace, human and divine, the light that "enlightens everyone who comes into this world" shines forth in its first and last radiance. He inaugurates the reign of a predestination, and the absolute manifestation of the Absolute. Is this, then, the end of history? No doubt: in him virtually everything is accomplished. But the honor and responsibility of actualizing its potential remains. The glory of the Monogenesis, or original unity, radiates a grace for which "those who have believed" will be hence responsible. They have received, only to give in their turn, and to build up, in a world whose resistances must be must served, the mystical body of Christ and the City of God. The victory of faith is but this fidelity to the one who has conquered the night.

II. THE WORD OF THE CROSS (EN CROIX)

This seems to me to be the general meaning of John's Prologue, as interpreted in an exegetical tradition that is represented, but not exclusively, by Catholicism. Modern exegesis would be more

reticent, I know, in certain quarters, in regard to this speculation that nourished ancient piety. It would denounce the pagan
intrusions of mythology that this theology took at face value in
order to retain, finally, in an existential interpretation, only the
historic event of the Word of God whose action encounters us
to call us into question. I do not intend to substitute the modern
for the ancient, or to open a discussion on the comparative merits of the two conceptions symbolized under the names of St.
Thomas and Bultmann. I am concerned with the effect of the
association provoked by bringing into relation the Johannine
Logos, thus understood, and the Logos of the Cross.

     1. However carefully we stress the Prologue's sources in the
Old Testament, it is difficult to escape the Greek atmosphere in
which it bathes, and which has been utilized by our theologians.
With their well-known intrepidity, they deduced consequences
that appeared to them to emerge implicitly from the text. They
contemplated, as did Paul, the Word of Wisdom; that wisdom
that they also "sought" because the Scripture authorizing them
led them clearly into this temptation. There they discovered the
beginnings of the great treatises relative to the Trinity, Creation,
and redemptive Incarnation. Little matter that they found
there, by retrospection, a dogmatic substance whose riches
were not promised by the sobriety of Paul's letter. They were
always able, and not without foundation, to find support there
for their constructive efforts. Thanks to a language whose metaphysical impregnation solicited their reflection, they invested
the wisdom of the Logos with so precise a noetic content that,
in the long run, its very precision could only awaken our suspicion. The God of whom they speak is, indeed, "Thought of the
Thought," that paradoxical identity that effaces all distance between subject and act, intellect and being, idea and its object.
The Word of splendor, pleroma of exemplary forms and divine
perfections, can from that point on only be consubstantial with
the supreme thinker, in spite of the problematic of relation that
assures their distinction. "Law of the world and norm of action,"
he is the substantial link that unifies the universe of things and
spirits. When he is made flesh, he unites in one person the
substantialized extremes that he mediates. Everything holds to-

gether within this conception. And I guard against minimizing its coherence.

2. The problem is elsewhere, in the astonishing contrast between the Word of the Cross who defies every wisdom, and this magnificent Word presented to us by a theology of subsisting thought. Are we destined, thereby, to the impossible task of uniting, in a single faith, two equally respectable sources that nourish it, without perceiving in them the sequential continuity that we desire? We will approach this serious question after having taken the exact measure of the conflict.

Some perhaps believe that no alternative is imposed because the Johannine Logos does not depend at all upon the elements integrated with it by centuries of philosophic commentaries. "All that," they add in a once-fashionable jargon, "comes from onto-theology."

I understand that the author of the Prologue could not have foreseen the exegeses it would inspire. Nonetheless, we must recognize that the text lends itself, independent of every artifice, to certain speculative developments. Attempts to tone down the Bible's Hellenic color only underscore, by contrast, the ineluctable presence of those very colors. It is not a question of an additive produced by the evil genie of metaphysicians. The protested excess is already there in the very word that gives the Jewish word, by the simple burden of translation, its new tonality and Western destiny.

As for "onto-theology," which is invoked in time and out of time, might we not best liberate ourselves from it by clarifying its status? According to the Kantian vocabulary, in the exact place in the Dialectic where examination of all speculative theology is introduced, onto-theology designates a sector of "transcendental theology" alongside cosmological theology, which must be constructed by recourse to experience of the world. It is characterized by a use of "pure concepts of understanding," but without any reference to the givens of a spontaneous or scholarly empiricism or to concepts of order of a physical or moral nature that are derived, according to the philosopher, from a strictly anthropological perspective. In sum, it occupies the place of the argument traditionally called "ontological." But according to Kant, this ontological argument expresses more than rational theology's tacit framework for all proof. Under a more or less technical form, it reveals the soul of all religious thought as it conceives of its God as the Most Real Being, whose infinite perfection and reason, as well as the cause of its existence, owe nothing to anyone. Would it be rash or offensive to think that on this point the Prologue's author shares the common condition, and that later theologians, when they reflected on the link between God and God's Word, did nothing but restore to that a priori all its expansive power?

3. Some will no doubt object that the God of the Bible, despite what has been said about the "metaphysics of the Exodus," escapes not only the argument, but also the very spirit, of ontotheology. What is decisive here would not be "thought" (or being) but the active and imperative Word, which confronts us with the radical possibilities of a choice under the species of light and shadow.

Does such an appeal to the Jewish source, that it foil the Greek, better safeguard that originality of faith that we would want to preserve? We may doubt it.

Despite the bonds that unite him to his origins, the apostle Paul gives preference to no one. Even though he recognizes a privileged situation, he maintains in this respect his decision's cutting edge. The Word of the Cross is under neither the sign of thought nor the sign of power or of will. Perhaps we must go further. Thought and will, which we like to oppose through multiple pairs of contraries—Hellenism-Judaism, Logos-Dabar—have indeed more than one common trait. Why is there not a "will of the will" or a "will of the self" symmetrical to "the thought of the thought" or "the thought of the self"? There is nothing to keep us from rediscovering, in the very domain of the will, a game of identities that annihilates, on the plane of thought, all distance between subject, act, product, thing, and principle. We would thus have, on the plane of will-Word, a similar succession of identities: willing subject = act of will = product of will (inclination toward self or auto-affection) = thing willed = principle of will (or "end").

The two ensembles, defined respectively by thought and will, are susceptible, under these conditions, to being applied, term by term, one to the other. The ensemble of departure (*pensée* or thought = P) comprises, for each of its elements, one image and only one in the ensemble of arrival (*vouloir* or will = V). By symbolizing, in the two cases, the subject by *s*, the product (*verbe* or *quasi-verbe*, or word or quasi-word) by *v*, the thing (thought or wished) by *r*, and the principle of act by *p*, we obtain the following schema, which illustrates well enough the relations of correspondence:

$$P: s = a, = v = r = p$$
$$V: s' = a' = v' = r' = p'$$

I will add, in complement, that the principle of arbitrary will rejoins, in the final instance, the absolute of the principle of reason, because, on one side or the other, whether it is a question of "reason of self" or "will of self" ("I will that which I am" or "I am that which I will"), a same Self of eminence presides over the absolutizing of the Absolute. But the folly and infirmity of the Word of the Cross signifies precisely the decline of these two absolutes. We cannot therefore privilege the one at the expense of the other. Johannine Logos, biblical Word, are they not then, for the perspective of faith, only retrospective languages?

III. THE TWO LANGUAGES

In the recent history of Christian theological development, we observe a sort of principle of alternation or compensation. The Greek dominance of certain epochs is diminished by multiplying exclusive references to the Old Testament. Everything goes on as if, since the time when the Logos of the Cross was solemnly proclaimed, it could be thought of only by projecting it into the past, into a double past. This oscillation betrays a constant imbalance. Is the Christian, then, *homo duplex*, one who can walk safely only by wobbling from one foot to another or resigning himself to a chronic bipolarity?

1. Such a strange condition provokes a question that seems to me neither superfluous nor superficial: How is it that the new

faith must flow either in the language of Greece or in that of Israel? By essence of necessity, must it not impugn the one and the other? How is it that the double negation, which is Pauline and staurological, is soon converted into more or less conjunctive compromises? To evoke an unfortunate bipolarity underscores an observation but does not explain it.

To clarify the question, while limiting myself to Christian responses, I will recall some judgments.

Most frequently, critics have bemoaned the Hellenic invasion, supposed to have repressed the emergence of specifically Christian categories. Platonism and Aristotelianism are supposed to have oriented toward impersonal idealism a scholastic theology which, under this foreign pressure, finally forgot its true God. To climb back up the slope, others have swung the pendulum back to the hour of Israel. Convinced that they will find in this cradle, if not the essential point of the Christian message, at least the most adequate language for faith's self-understanding, they read in the ancient Bible the indispensable preambles for comprehending the New Covenant: prophecy, Word-will, the history of salvation. More recently, some have wanted to take up the theme again with a different stress. They are concerned with the voice of the prophets, more mindful of the defense of the poor against the rich and powerful than the reaffirmation of the unique God, Lord of the world and master of history. For some of them, Jesus takes up and amplifies the prophetic protest.

Such diverse claims bear witness to a moving search for identity, and even more, to the Christian's fundamental difficulty of being what she was always meant "to be." They invite us to consider more deeply a generic situation from which the newest movements can not extricate themselves.

2. It is a fact, lamentable or not, that Christianity was destined from the beginning to speak Hebrew and Greek. We do not know the revolutions that created each part of their lexicon and syntax. The sciences themselves have completed, by natural language, their artificial symbolism. For the best reasons, this recourse was imposed on a faith addressed to all, which, to make itself understood, had to borrow from the different mi-

lieus that encountered its diffusive power. The new wine demands the ancient bottle that contained it. And if it had to break it, as it had to, it did so after having used it. The contaminations we complain about in one way or another are inscribed in its destiny. The yet unheard-of categories that we want, if we can speak thus of categories, can flourish only through recovering a previous discourse and modifying its resonances.

At the level of simple "transduction," this power of innovation has frequently been noted. Translations do not reproduce, in their transduction, a simple equivalent. Through their turns and their inflections they produce another world. For the Cross to be transmitted efficaciously, it is also vulnerable to a twofold deformation: the ancient by the new and the new by the ancient. The early language was able to carry it only by submitting it, in turn, to the shock of a forced semantic. The repetition we bemoan, which is not a duplication at all, thus defines one of these conditions of viability.

But there is more. To understand the exceptional dominance of biblical language in the kerygma of the Cross, we must recall that Israel is the mother earth, not reducible to one simple possibility, among others, of communication. By way of retrospection, and under the form of virtual possibility, its history becomes the prehistory of an event. Indeed, the preaching of the first days constantly projects the innovating present into a past that prefigures it. This apologetic function of reading has been maintained until our day. It responds to a vital exigency. But it is not enough, if the new preaching is to have a future, that it be proclaimed in its own original specificity. It risks sounding schizophrenic if it does not refer back to that context from which it emerged, however improbably. The artifice of an obscure pre-existence, whose future form is traced by the shadows through the course of ages, obeys a principle of reason or, if you will, an ideology of justification. The ancient covenant that the preacher solicits bears witness to the new, and refutes in advance those who would not recognize, in the light it diffuses, the definitive truth of a bygone past. This is an exorbitant conceit, no doubt, that somewhat compromises the innovative instance that it vaunts, but it has the incontestable advantage of balancing the initial rupture with an intelligible corrective and satisfying the good conscience of faith.

Is an oscillation so characteristic of Christian thought the sign of a congenital problem that can be remedied only by the pure and simple return to one or another of our two sources? Or, inversely, is it rather the proof or sign of a richness difficult to master, whose very excess is betrayed to the vicissitudes of an alternation that sustains hope for a definitive synthesis indefinitely postponed to the future?

IV. The Future of Theology

This last response, which some would deem the only one possible, presupposes that Christian faith must have a content at once specific and all-encompassing. The Cross becomes, for them, the banner of an identity that affirms itself in proud awareness of the unique and its fullness. The Johannine Logos, which by its divine excellence is the substantial link that joins the universe of things and the world of history, prolongs its incarnation in a visible body that simultaneously knows, from a knowledge of faith, the center of being and, in the twofold sense of the word, the "end" of becoming. Its unicity is but the expression of a totality which, lest it betray its name, tolerates outside of itself only diminutives of its "virtue" or branches of its power.

1. Such a conception is justified primarily through the authority of a long dogmatic and disciplinary tradition whose claims are explicated in our ancient treatise, *De vera religione.* It responds, moreover, to the necessities of faith's social existence, which concretize, in their fashion, the metaphysical axiom by which "nothing exists which is not determined, specific, individualized."

However reasonable, these appeals to common sense suggest a double observation.

On the one hand, the elements integrated within the doctrine of faith, taken in themselves, possess nothing specifically Christian. When we enumerate them one after the other, we can always uncover, more or less precisely, a "pagan" origin. The concepts or images we are concerned with are found in the common fount of religious representations. Surely this banal observation is not sacrilegious.

On the other hand, we cannot deny that these "elements," by way of a secular elaboration, enter into relatively new semantic complexes. In this respect, their Christian recovery is more or better than a repetition. It is precisely because of this original contribution, which unites in its complexity a "diversity" borrowed from multiple sources, that people could believe in the miracle of a Christian synthesis, in which the best that had been sought in the uncertainties of the past would be gathered together. This is an understandable and perhaps necessary illusion, whose fervor has nourished a confessional pride that has served us as patriotism for a long time.

2. It must be admitted, however, that pride in the unique and its immense ownership tends to efface the relation of faith to its origin. The judgment of the Cross hardly favors such a hearty conviction. Rather, it discourages all exaltation of a fullness that would condense within itself the fine flowering of the real. The decision or break to which it calls us hardly suits a "realism" whose prestige crowns a community owing its name to the lacerated body of Christ. If I did not fear the pun that Claudel allowed, I would say that this *name* is first a *no.*

It is thus in this judgment of the Cross that a solution to the real or apparent conflict between Johannine Logos and Pauline Logos must rest.

Of what order is this judgment? If jargon can be excused, it seems that the Kantian distinction between "determining" and "reflective" judgment helps clarify matters. The judgment of the Cross is not in the order of a "determining" judgment. In other words, it brings to us no new knowledge of God that would permit us to determine his being, nor prize of predicates to add to the attributes discerned by earlier religions in order to englobe the first and subordinate them to his incommensurable eminence. It is thus that we have interpreted Paul's rejection of the two reductive temptations whose seductiveness he dreads. These two references are only exemplars of all that can be said in religious language, in human words. The cutting edge of this staurological rupture is brought to bear on this totality, virtually present to his thought. Henceforth every desire to magnify the new by crowning it with an *et cetera* of perfections, however well-intentioned, only drains off the uncompromising energy of this initial rupture. In no way can the judgment of the Cross be, in a passage to the limit, an infinite judgment that would spell out, on the same transcendent subject, the interminable and ordained successions of its theological fulgurations. The poverty of the new God rejects this litanical superabundance and reduces it, in order to do justice to mystery, by a coincidence of opposites that throw the enduring shadow of contradiction upon this solar glory. If arithmetic helps here, I dare to say that subtraction is more discrete and radical than addition.

3. The judgment of the Cross yields us no new determination; it adds no burst of light upon the divine *doxa*. Of what, then, does it consist? The term "reflective," which I proposed in a first approximation, says at once too much and too little. Too much to the extent that it designates a thought in the strict sense, obviously foreign to the Sign that interrogates us. Too little, if it designates only a secondary consideration, or the scientific indifference of "the disinterested observer." I am holding on to it, however, because it expresses in some way what must be the attitude of the "new man" called the Son of Man. First, it indicates to us, through this taking back that takes us to the gift, the necessary asceticism of a necessary distanciation. For how sweet it is to adhere for time immemorial to what brings to us only detachment, to what signifies the rigor and participates in the radicality of death. This distance is not the same, however, as pure and simple annihilation. The old man in us always conceals his idols. And in every way, the horror of the void elicits an endless play of representations through individual or social pressures. It would be useless to deny it or exorcise this specter by the simple magic of verbal negation. I am, without a doubt, wrong to condemn the "old man." The Cross does not exempt us from the human condition or from the need, also very human, to clothe the "naked god" with our history, turbu-

lent or calm, where values and prejudice, weakness and generosity, are inextricably mixed.

4. Faith must, consequently, inhabit the world and give to its God—I risk this bold way of speaking—the being he has not. Theology, in its subordinate but indispensable role, can only be inserted in the same movement. It must be "in the world," and in the manner proper to it. I have tried, above, to entrust to theology, as future tasks, certain questions too often neglected by the dogmatic tradition. But theology must go beyond this problematic if it is to realize its plenitude. And it is here that the Johannine Logos reasserts itself, if not in its substance, at least in its functions. For theology, in its fundamental impulse that makes it "in," "toward," and "about" the Cross, measures up to its mission only to the extent that it espouses the mission of the Word: *sponsa Verbi*. Like the Word, theology will be light of the world of faith and of the Cross. Light, that is to say, "link," or better still, according to the beautiful expression of the past, "phrase" and "syntax" of multiple representations through which, at a given moment, the Sign of the Cross is objectified on our earth. Yet the logic of theology is not limited to this imperative of rigor. It is not enough to enchain, in theological propositions, the predicates or denominations through which the divine is actualized at a certain time. These "divine names" sum up a development, crystallize a result. Lest we erect them into absolutes, then, we must submit them to an elucidation that clarifies their meaning and bearing. This is a task to be constantly renewed, because every acquisition trembles in contingency, carried along as it is by the exotic flux of faith. Finally, as we too easily forget, we can only determine the meaning of a language by plunging it back into the individual and social practice for which it was normative. This pragmatic dimension corresponds to the phase of incarnation, which, in the Prologue, concludes the dialectic of the journey. Perhaps, moreover, the final stage must in reality be the first. Whatever ordering principle we choose, the organic correlation of the elements remains essential. It returns to theology to maintain and promote the relationships that make a world, a dwelling for the Cross. It is by this supple and exigent logic, knowing the price of determi-

nations without ignoring their fragility, that theology can still exercise among us the essential functions of a Logos.

5. However indispensable its role, this determining judgment is only half the task. If it is impossible to leave our world, it is no less necessary not to be its prisoner. Therefore, the freedom of faith, and of theology, cannot, in its reflective judgment, ignore the virtue of the Cross, which repeats in face of every new form of expression of being the interrogation immanent to the Sign of contradiction. In this respect we must not yield to bias. We too easily look ironically upon the past to discard it in the rubble of history. This facile gesture believes itself to be free because it sacrifices to the present. Such is the dogmatism of a new "common sense," often more sectarian than the ancient. Theological courage would never, under the guise of independence profit from such an abdication. Instead of particularizing the Cross it would universalize it; recalling that we have no permanent dwelling in any time or place. In this respect, present and future dwell under the same sign as the past. They obey without any possible discrimination that detached and questioning rigor that characterizes, this side of what can properly be called knowledge, the ironic "I think" of faith.

This meditation on the tasks of a theology that goes out from the Cross in order to return there after having created its world, allows us to respond to the initial question: Are the Johannine and Pauline Logos compatible? Or do they indeed condemn us to that perpetual division that seems to rend the Christian conscience?

The response is pertinent only if we sustain the diversity of levels within their real unity. Determination and reflection contradict each other only if we block them out in the same dimension.

The Johannine Logos, at least in the constructive theology inspired and prolonged by it, unfolds in a world of images and concepts whose place of origin can be located. For us, it is doubly precious. On the one hand, it means that the silence of the ineffable makes itself understood in a word; that faith, in its very fidelity, offers its word of intelligence; and that the Cross itself also merits its word or its fable, if we no longer relegate it to a transcendence whose illusoriness we have already denounced. On the other hand, it gathers together, in an organized ensemble, the rudiments of a creed whose different moments reflect the unity of the universe and history. In thus fixing in an anterior language a first theory of faith, it thus invites us tacitly to the same bold gesture. For we must construct or reconstruct, under conditions that are never the same, a worldly body that shelters, in the course of our days, the one necessary thing that is entrusted to us.

That call to creation, which we wish were more often heard, is ceaselessly crossed by a critical instance that comes from the other Logos. The Word on the Cross renders a judgment on the chain of determinations that reduces their pretense to be eternal without excluding their service. Determination and reflection, Johannine Logos and Pauline Logos, far from contradicting one another, must therefore sustain one another in composing, one after the other, their respective alterities. It is a difficult equilibrium, ceaselessly interrupted for the sake of an anarchic contestation or rigid inertia. Whatever form this hardening takes—whether we linger on irreversible definitions in which the flash of a fallen star forever shines, or take delight in a constant refusal whose impotence accommodates itself to anything whatever—in either way, the cross is betrayed, since, by excess or by default, it is exiled from our earth.

The judgment of the Cross unites the resolute decision, of concept and action, which risks being firmly inscribed; and the "margin of a smile"—that ironic sense of detachment that keeps it from being imposed upon by any solemnity of establishment. It is a matter not of paralyzing bipolarity but of a decisive march whose support and thrust are confirmed by their reciprocal necessity. For the Cross to exist in the victory of faith, it must assume the weight of a reality in which flow together the present and past and future uncertainties of a heritage, but also the morning breeze that shatters in the freshness of its passage the mortal and cherished forms of our creations.

8

The Cross Today

DOES THE ADVERB "today" *(aujourd'hui)*, which we sometimes transform into the radiant substantive "the beautiful day" *(le bel aujourd'hui)*, still make sense when applied to the Cross? Precisely what does this modish, overused word denote? Is it that moment that the logician attempts to define, or a dark and nebulous "now," best left to situation analysts? And in this latter case, what must be said? In this milieu of fluidity, which envelops us and every decisive word, the most optimistic seek the joy of a less monitored "elsewhere," whatever its historical content. The most cautious, however, suspect here the opening of another horizon, yet unknown to them but calling into question the most certain foundations.

Would the Sign of contradiction, as well as the tradition that has partially carried it, be swept along by the same autumnal wind? Or, strong and purified in its powerlessness, would it stand strong against the sea, like the unyielding rock that would be our fortress and defense "forever"? As they are spoken, these questions, which could be endlessly multiplied, betray an anxiety before the future that diminishes heroic courage of conviction. I raise them without any agenda of modernization or apologetics. And I do not care to answer them. No one, it seems to me, can be sure that the Cross has a youthful and timely present. Nothing promises that it has a future to dispose of. I leave such crystal-gazing and guesswork to historians and prophets. For my part, I would prefer to take up the Cross as it has appeared to me in the shadows, in order to hurl it, uncovered, into the bitter waters of our inept struggles. By way of a divergent reading that once opened up to me the coral gardens of an essential remembrance, I will venture a commentary on some texts that also arise from an immemorial folly.

1. On that slope, perhaps leading nowhere, I used to con-

template with awe the "mount of beatitudes," of *macarismes,* as used to be said in a Greek expression reserved almost exclusively for Church matters. The "blessed one" hailed by these jubilant exclamations does not stand on a statue's pedestal, supported by a founding justification, but exists only in tears, in persecution, clothed with a poverty that illumines hunger and thirst for justice. Plato had already dreamed, in the *Republic,* of a just one stripped of every appearance, who "always appeared to be criminal." The Platonic "wretch" is also the "most happy of all." The Beatitudes, then, are not the private property of any institution or specific tradition. Moreover, such concerns about the first owner are bothersome. They are the concern of exegetes and theologians. Perhaps the modest sign of the one thing necessary is a gentle irony that has little regard for brand names and petty wars of distribution. In the final analysis, what does it matter who was first author or mother earth? These burning texts have consumed their origin. They are, for us, origin and orientation. We receive them as such. Enigmatic as the oracle, they express neither the truth of scientific adequation, nor conformity to an exemplary idea. What, then, do they say?

We seek a place for them within our categories. From what language do they arise? Thwarted, we review the prevailing distinctions: constative, performative, imperative. In what time and mode do we place what they propose? Is it even a question of a proposition, unless we understand by this expression some "leap" or élan that throws us off our beaten paths? Such is, indeed, the impression they leave with us. They invite us to go beyond that much discussed "function of the real" or "reality principle." Do they lead us to a royal utopian kingdom or to the space of dreams that is commonly called "the country of nightmares"?

No doubt, we have long known that "they overcome the world." They engage us in a paradoxical non-place that gathers all those signed with the secret mark of perpetual indigence into the nonexistent class of beloved children of misfortune. Singular paradise, the rational animal adds the prevailing and more or less scholarly critique of the underclass to her natural distrust!

But in this case, are we really talking about hard to imagine people who sometimes nourish the imbalance of alienation?

The Beatitudes are only descriptive expressions that can be substituted for the substantive "Gospel." The suggestion of the future characterizing these consoling words is thus an illusion. Like the Gospel, the Beatitudes are already in the midst of us, in us, the promise of a magnificent possibility that coincides with its realization. And that is why they effect a true reversal. While happiness is popularly thought of as the crown of a deliberate action, its immanent direction, finality, and realization, the evangelical beatitude of the Cross transcends all teleology. This blessedness is not the "for what" for which we work and must merit. Rather than crowning a history, it constitutes that history's beginning. Like the Johannine Word, it is the principle of a genesis. From it proceed the virtuous acts and practical knowledge that our psycho-sociologies of the human act have tried to analyze through the model of an orderly free will, dialectically extended through the three well known stages of intention, instrumental mediation, and joyful fulfillment. To understand it, we must ascend again the common path of a certain understanding. If one seeks a distant analogy with a philosophical text, perhaps the last theorem of Spinoza's *Ethics* sums it up best: "Beatitude is not the recompense of virtuous strength but virtue itself. It is not because we restrain our desires that we enjoy it; on the contrary, it because we enjoy it that we can master them."

Should not this last marvelous theorem in the order of exposition be, ontologically, the first? For the Gospel of the Cross, which does not burden us with these subtleties, the primordial in itself is also the orientation that enlightens us and dwells within us.

Yet the similarity examined demands a corrective that would distinguish the dissimilarity. The Sign of contradiction turns us away from a substantial fullness that covers the source of beatitude with an infinity of attributes. Of course, in either case, our joy must remain if we are to dominate the vicissitudes of time. But if we ask where this joy dwells, the answers are diametrically opposed. The Cross announces from the outset its méontological difference. The conversion it calls for asks us to orient ourselves no longer toward the splendors of a totality where excellences are accumulated. The rupturing Word mortifies that subtle greed that adds to the positive in order to elevate, above the world and the human, the apotheosis of the world and the human. The way of riches and ease is henceforth only the most secret and deadly temptation. Faith's demon denounces its illusory generosity. It is not in these crystal palaces that our most beautiful dreams are sheltered or our true joy rests.

In their provocative form, the beatitudes are but commentary on this decision. They do not launch a scholarly critique of our certitudes or our pleasures. They simply define, by the trace of their golden arrows, the other place that our heart inhabits. And it is from this high place that, through a sort of retrospection, the shared places of our shared evidences appear as they are. Is not the harshest judgment the one that leaves behind us, this side of the élan it could no longer contain, the presumed obstacle that we abandon to its hypothetical past?

Would such an austerity still be compatible with that joy of which it was said, "It surpasses all understanding"? Does it not open before us the pure and simple void? Is the interior superabundance that we associate invincibly with beatitude identical with the despairing uniformity that effaces all distinctions, with the very substance of ennui?

This uneasiness is not surprising. It marks the return of the real, too quickly disqualified, avenging a sham indifference. The world we would forget, we might add, lies always in the background of our forgetting. Surreptitiously, despite what we say, it adorns with its colors and forms that unclothed Cross about which we pretend to boast. It is always Being that we cannot overcome.

Such a language is not unknown to us. It surprises us less since the Pauline challenge gains its cutting edge by this very reference; and beatitude, if it is not of this world, must also and necessarily dwell in this world. A difference does not impose a separation. The common sense reaction can therefore only be expected and understood. But does it follow that we must join together what we are forbidden to separate? Such is the true question that the Sign sets before us; more exactly, that it invites us to ask, as if it found in us a tacit complicity that, even before the question, prepares a place for it in our inner space, in that original void that anticipates the question and the answer. For it is within us—in this empty space, in this "seed of non-being" evoked above—that the Cross has established its dwelling place forever, even before being traced upon the horizon of the world; and it is within us that the judgment which judges the world "before the world comes to be" is pronounced. In this "nothingness," battered by the flow of beings and things but holding them in respect, resides the supreme freedom that repeats upon every massive presence, night and day, the question of the shameful Sign. The mount of the Beatitudes is that rarefied air of the heights; or that depth of the soul that is the poor name and the "non" of the new god. It would be vain to seek elsewhere for the joy in which faith exults. To preserve it from illusion, we are always tempted to give it a precise content that invites the corresponding illusion of a solid verification, in the certitude of a necessary "fulfillment." Such an obsessive fear of losing the world is as natural and conformed to our condition as the perception of the broken staff in the mirror of the waters. But is fear of losing the world the surest means of gaining it?

2. The joy of the Beatitudes knows, however, that "there is something else," and that this other merits more and better than a distracted attention. That distant height, which the spiritual symbolize in the hollow of the rock, is not hollowed out in a solitude where the unique savors the eternal delectation of its private property. "The substantial action" that does nothing would betray its germinal power if it were nothing but the eternal repose of tired souls. From the other side of the mountain, the unconditional call resounds once more to the servants of the kingdom. For the God who is beyond the forms of being, of wisdom, and of power, far from dispensing us from this body of the world and of humanity to render homage in spirit, requires these attributes in order to come among us *in truth*. It is precisely because he is nothing of that which is that he must *become*. But this "becoming" necessarily passes through the face of the other. Nothing is more disconcerting in this regard than

the last judgment according to St. Matthew (25,31–46). At the hour of truth that sounds the final decline of the idols, in that flash of lightening that concentrates a life upon the one thing necessary, what we would have thought essential is not what finally matters. The last day is, in a certain way, the triumph of the everyday. The "blessed of the Father" hear then, as inheritors of the kingdom, the revelatory Word: "I was hungry and you gave me to eat; I was thirsty and you gave me to drink; I was a stranger and you visited me, a prisoner and you came to see me." Those awaiting the sentence make no appeal to those things that common religious sense would have deemed indispensable: cult, adoration, absolute submission to a transcendent Truth. The elect themselves seem not to understand: "Lord, when did we see you hungry and nourish you, thirsty and quench your thirst, a stranger and welcome you, naked and clothe you, sick or prisoner and come to see you?" This most reasonable question shows us how far from faith is a certain image of the Supreme. The response is as neat as we would wish: "Truly I say to you, in so far as you did this to one of the least of these brethren, you did it to me" (Jerusalem Bible). Strange condition of this god who seems to acquire a Self only through these little ones who do not exist, and whose essence seems to consist in the very possibility of a face! Would the most distant also be the most near? Or is it that we know neither near nor far? Are not the poor, in their non-being, the shadow on our earth of that kenosis Paul celebrates as that yet unseen (inouie) future?

Is this disconcerting God, therefore, only the infinite possibility of disturbing us? What remains certain is this: the beatitude of the Cross, so similar, in its starkness, to the everyday prose of misfortune, is also the awakening of an inquietude and the exigency of an irrepressible "procession." It is not a question of an exodus that would exile us from fundamental joy, as if, in the retrospective resentment that condemns it, it would represent the original sin from which one must excuse oneself or be accused. Nor is this necessary "procession" the haughty condescension that lets fall from the table of the rich the crumbs of the banquet. It is not the contagious compassion that would offer to the unfortunate only the emotional witness of a common suffering. This psychologizing imagery, close parent of a tiresome virtue, substitutes an axiom of sloth for an historic imperative of realization. For the unbelievable or impossible commands the most down to earth realism: "I was naked and you clothed me." The history of the Cross is defined by the humblest gestures: dress, nourish, shelter, quench. In such banality, it is not surprising that the irresponsible faithful fear that the economy of faith has been reduced to vulgar materialism. Indeed, the intransigent paradox signifies the necessity of giving, to that which has no face, that face of light radiant with the joy of the beginning: *fiat lux*. From the nothingness of the Origin, a universe must arise so that Being, in all its expansion, will be not only its trace but the "praise of its glory." I am aware that the lilies of the field, which are proposed to us as a model, neither "toil nor spin." But before the world becomes that dream of innocence in which the gaze of the seventh day reposes, the Cross must be dug into our soil to disturb our complacent equilibriums. Then, but only then, the world will be for the Son of Man the flower of his Passion.

Yet I do not claim that the equation of a new world is already fixed in the stars, or that simply examining the Cross will uncover there the premises of a future conclusion. The Word that proceeds from the Cross is not an immediate given to be read in inspired scriptures. Nothing is written on the Sign of contradiction if not the need for us to trace, on the void from which grace is given us, the straight or crooked line of our paths. On that indefinitely open horizon, faith's earthly concern is to bring forth the rigorous Word confided to the work of its hands. "The Son of Man is come to serve and not to be served." Such is the spirit of our action. But this spirit, which we sometimes abuse in order to resist its difficult truth, does not dispense us, in the name of fervor, from either the logic of action or the boldness of a course whose failures or falls we cannot calculate. I do not know what "the future of Christianity" will be. But for that future to be worth knowing, if it is to be an object of knowledge someday, we must first make it be and have the courage to be. The rest "will be given us by excess."

This "rest," or this excess, is not only that which is "unhoped for," implicit in every fearless action. It dwells like the glow-worm in the grass of our meadows, in the noblest as well as the humblest actions. This accompaniment softly and quietly rules the ordering of our intentions. The Gospel of the Cross reserves no precise name for it. It lies hidden in the innocent qualifier that tempers the dangerous substantive in which our vanity hides: "useless servant." What a singular if not contradictory expression (what would a servant be without usefulness?), which joins in this subject the right of negation and the affirmation of its function! Yet it is not a question here of conflicting adjectives. Considered more closely, the adjective determines nothing. It indicates in another language a reflection or a return that places at a distance that which it mirrors, in order to preserve the image of beatitude from the taint of the idol or rigidity of the statue. Legitimate concern for the coming of the Kingdom on earth risks, indeed, submerging faith in feverish work that is the more exultant the more it seems disinterested. The judgment of uselessness does not simply add a corrective to an all too human satisfaction or to a feverish failure to confront an exhausting problem. It claims to be radical. In extending to the ideally realized totality of all our enterprises, it casts on each and all of them the fraternal shadows of freedom and death. It is this improbable liaison that I want to stress.

The freedom in question has nothing to do with an abstract questioning that is intoxicated by "negation for its own sake." It exercises upon a determined result a precise and repeated negation that is the execution of the "to die" *(mourir)*. I do, indeed, say "to die," and not "death," at least if the latter is understood as the inevitable fact of a definitive and irreversible limit. Although we are not lords over death thus understood, we are always masters of an "act of dying," which is not the external power of an absolute obstacle but the other face of a freedom whose strength is more than the play of its productions. If the term were not a cliché, I would speak of "mortification," though not the mortification that initially applies the asceticism of desire to the progressive extinction of all appetite. As we know well, the "spiritual combat" is not without danger: by desiring to liberate the self it risks reinforcing its central position and exacerbating its prestige. The forgetfulness of self effected by "the act of dying" bears first upon a relatively foreign body. It bears less upon the "self" *(soi)* than on the "self's" *(sien)*: with the heady undulation of the "self," which traces the ripples of renewed exultation around our works. Liberating mortification is nothing other than this permanent possibility of detachment. Might the best example of it be the serene objectivity of the scholar who proposes a hypothesis so as to submit it to the test of eventual falsification? Or would it be, on another level, the universal doubt of the philosopher who claims to know from experience the fragility of every proof, however seemingly indestructible?

These two cases we have invoked, relating them perhaps more than is suitable, illustrate a demand for integrity that we must respect. Yet they do not recover the movement of retreat and disappropriation designated by the term "to die." Perhaps, it is true, our familiar evidences, personal or collective, respond badly (even and especially when they appeal to an invincible light) to a demand for lucidity. But they ascend to the asceticism of the "to die" only if they constitute, in the name of private property, the substance or the inalienable essence that defines a confession, a party, an individuality, in their uniqueness. Must we then, one may object, dissolve, in the name of the Cross, the only reality that can truly exist so that we may know its singular and unrepeatable originality? Such an abnegation would be equivalent to suicide or the foolish primacy of an illusory abstraction.

Of course, we can rightly protest against the anonymous grayness in which "that which alone has the right to exist" would disappear. But the folly of the Cross identifies itself with neither abstract theory nor the triumph of the impersonal. Rather, it appeals to an inalienable singularity, conscious of what it has and what it is, in order to invite it to refer itself back to the null point that is the place or the non-place of its beatitude. The shadow of this nonexistent point thus projects, on its being and its having, the original nothingness that returns them to their source. It and it alone, because it is beyond being, wisdom, and power, can confer on the soul the freedom of such a folly. As for suicide, whose menace is recalled to us, nothing excludes the possibility that, in certain given conditions and aside from solutions of despair, the decision of a serene conscience could inscribe the act of suicide within the logic of an unconditional service. Indeed, what prevents the price of life we invoke from no longer compensating for the enormous burden it places on others? Or what prevents the servant, faithful to the end to the one who is served, from abolishing, in a supreme gesture of abandonment and love, that "body of death" that is offered from that moment on in sacrifice? "Useless servant," but servant all the same, he obeys in this act of ultimate judgment the Cross that speaks to him in one last night on that bald mountain, where it once was said, "I put my soul in your hands."

Thus the modalities of distanciation may vary. The essential point remains, at its depth, what was called freedom. Yet one might ask if the boldness of this exegesis does not conceal the fear of another question. Might insistence on the "to die" be not the middle way taken to avoid the problem of death? In other words, might the Cross not shroud death itself under the power of the "to die"? And, in this case, how would it be possible to reverse this irreversible?

The radicality of the Sign of contradiction hardly seems to favor nostalgia for immortality, with its vital egoism and other-worldly illusion. Moreover, no dialectic, however ingenious, persuades us that a "negation of the negation" can knock down, by artifice, the wall that awaits us. And we have hardly more confidence in promises of evolution and process. Even if we accord them only a relative value, they indicate to us less the way to follow than the traps to avoid. If "to die on the cross" retains its mastery of death itself, it is because it pronounces on this irreducible death the judgment that deprives it of its irreducibility. What constitutes this ultimate function of the "to die"?

We would perhaps like the "to die" to dissolve magically into a simple appearance of the brutality of an ultimate fact. But if it were but one more distraction from the inevitable, it would rejoin in its shallowness the soporific virtue of consoling sermons. I allow that, humans being human, the overcoming of appearances has always been the categorical imperative that makes that more than reasonable animal a being of interrogation and defiance. But appearances do not evaporate into a chimera. The Christian defiance of death, or further, the "to die of death" taken seriously, cannot dissolve the terrible sensible reality submitted to its verdict. This side of all bravado, it demands that we take the measure of its radicality. For death, we need not repeat, is imposed as the "radical" fact. Nonetheless, a fact, whatever it be, and it would be radical, never has the simplicity of an atom of sensation or a shock to which we must only submit. As the most diverse sciences have convinced us, death imposes itself only within a cadre of intelligibility that gives it its impact and real import. It is necessary, then, that death, in the light of the "dying on the Cross," be illumined with a new intelligibility. Inseparable from the world, whose ephemerality it restores, death participates by confirming its irreducible unyieldingness. That is why the judgment of the Cross does not dissociate the world and death. From this it follows that if the faith the Cross inspires "victory over the world," it must, through the same movement, be victory over death. But this double victory is itself possible only if "there is something in us that does not flow from world," though we participate by our very being in the movement of nature and history that carries us. Only on this condition can the "to die of death" be thought. The judgment of the Cross thus returns us to that "nothingness" that is not of the world, so that even while we dwell in the world we are not submerged in it. We have tried to name the better part. It cannot be distinguished from the kenosis of the Cross; from that "non-being" in which, in the same "in-difference," the soul of the faithful and the God of her faith are indissolubly united. From this second perspective, without losing its sting, death is ultimately intelligible and sensible only in its relation to that "nothingness" par excellence, which it schematizes and articulates. It achieves the conversion of all things to their origin. Far from being, as we first advanced, a "phenomenon of the world," death envelops the world in its shadow and consumes in this "reflection," or reflux, its respiration or "spirit."

"To render the spirit": thus is the transitivity of the "to die" translated in the language of the Gospel and everyday life. Death, the last breath, places upon this rendering the seal of irreversibility, and convinces us that all is done. The last word of Christ on the cross rectifies and makes clear: "All is finished." That word, uttered in a loud voice and in the torment of thirst, underscores, in the hour of transit, the passage from end to accomplishment, from death to the "to die," which "returns the spirit" to its dwelling place. Is the spirit of the Cross then this passage? Or that breath of which we know neither whence it comes nor whence it goes"? And this mobility that leaves one free and that "to die" consecrates; this "being toward" which refers all that is to "that which is not," would never think of abandoning the unmovable and quiescent beatitude which indwells, in the nakedness of the soul, those poor of Christ who know, in giving up the spirit, where their treasure lies.

The Cross joins together beatitude, service, and death. That strange trinity remains yet to be thought. Are we more advanced at the end of this journey than at the beginning? And would it not have been better to trace in the sand, with foot or hand, this Sign, more paltry than the Southern Cross, which pierces the heart with a point of interrogation, a point that both inflames and leaves a mark of sorrow?

APPENDIX

Being, God and the Poetics of Relation: Interview of Stanislas Breton by Richard Kearney

Richard Kearney: Your philosophical journey has been wide ranging. You have published works on such diverse topics as neoplatonism, Thomism, Marxism, phenomenology, logic and poetics. What would you consider to be the unifying threads in this tapestry of intellectual interests?

Stanislas Breton: First, I would say that my philosophical journey is related to my biographical one. My early upbringing and education in a rural community in La Vendée certainly had a significant impact on my subsequent thinking; it determined my later leanings towards a certain philosophical *realism.* This perhaps accounts somewhat for the fact that in the doctorate I presented to the Sorbonne, *Approches phénoménologiques de l'idée d'être,* I tended to see the key metaphysical concept, "Being as Being," in terms of the four elements of the concretely experienced, real world: earth, fire, water, air. Strange as it may sound, the monastic experience of my early years in a Passionist seminary, which I entered at the age of fifteen, also corresponded in some way to my conceptualization of *Being as Being:* this decisive concept thus emerged as both a monastic desert and an all-englobing shelter of the four elements of nature. Philosophy begins, I believe, in the life-world. So it is not very surprising that our understanding of Being should be colored by our lived experience, by the formative *images* of our being in the world. This conviction predisposed me, of course, to a *phenomenological* approach to philosophy; it also confirmed my belief that a poetics of imagination is an indispensable dimension of genuine thinking.

Kearney: I think that your conviction would be shared by many of the phenomenologists. Sartre, Camus and Merleau-Ponty all spoke of the decisive way in which their concretely *lived experience* affected their subsequent understanding of Being, which they saw as a "universal" reflection on their "particular," prereflective existence. But what philosophical or intellectual influences on your thinking would you consider to be of primary importance?

Breton: The earliest intellectual influence I can recall was the Latin language—the way in which it was used in the seminary with a scholastic emphasis on professional rigor and prepositional distinction: *ex, in, ad, de* and so on. This language of *relations*, which Lévinas calls "transitive language," greatly influenced my doctorate in Rome entitled *L'Esse* in *et l'esse* ad *dans la métaphysique de la relation*. This scholastic logic of relations was the second major influence on my philosophical imagination for it raised the fundamental question of how man can be *in* Being (immanence) and still be said to be moving *towards* it (transcendence). Once applied to the work of St. Thomas, it opened up the whole problematic of the "operations" of ontological immanence with its crucial theological implications for our understanding of the Trinity: How does the Son belong to the Father and the Father to the Son through the agency of the Spirit? I would almost say that my mature interest in philosophy sprang from theological questions which theology itself could not answer. For example, the *Being-in* relation provided an explanation of the unity of the Three Persons of the Trinity, while the distinction and difference between the Three could be understood in terms of the intentional or transitive relation of the *Being-towards*. The Spirit could thus be interpreted as a twofold relation: (i) the perpetual attraction between the Father and the Son; and (ii) the power of movement and carrying-beyond (*meta-pherein*), which refuses the finite limits of proprietal possession and makes the Trinity an *infinite relation*.

This theology of operations also has important implications for our understanding of the Incarnation. The "substantialist" theology of the Councils, which spoke of the two natures in one, seemed to me insufficient in so far as it privileged the notion of *substance* over that of *function* or *relation*. The dynamic relation of the Being-towards category struck me as being closer to the Biblical language of transitivity. God as a Being-in-itself, as an identical substance, cannot be thought by us; we can only know or speak about God in terms of His relation to us, or ours to Him.

My interest in the theology of operations soon led to an interest in the philosophy of mathematical relations. When I was captured by the Germans during the War, I had three books in my bag: Bochenski's *Elements of Mathematical Logic*, Brunschvicg's *Modality of Judgment* and Hamelin's *The Principle Elements of Representation*. Another work which deeply fascinated me at the time was Bertrand Russell's *Introduction à la philosophie mathématique*, where he outlined a sophisticated philosophy of descriptive relations. In short, what I appreciated most in these thinkers was their analysis of the operative terms of relation—prepositions such as *in, towards*, and the conjunctions *as, as-if*, which I called "those little servants of the Lord." I believe they are not only the indispensable accompaniment of all thought but also the secret messengers of the philosophical future.

Kearney: Could you elaborate on your philosophical transition from the initial question of *Being as Being* (an ontology of the four elements of nature) to the correlative question of *Being-in* and *Being-towards* (a metaphysics of relation)?

Breton: I was drawn towards the metaphysical problematic of relations in order to try to understand not just what Being is as such, but how it relates to man or accounts for the way in which the Three Divine Persons relate to each other. The relation of Being-towards constitutes the element of metaphor or metamorphosis, that which assures the infinite movement of existence as a passing over from one phase to the next; it is that which compels us to continually alter our concepts, making each one of us a "being in transit."

The relation of Being-in, by contrast, is that *élément neutre* which draws together and unifies existence; it is that which founds our notion of ontological self-identity. In the *Metaphysics*, Aristotle refers to this principle when he states that the addition of Being or the One to something changes nothing. Being added to man adds nothing. For Being is not a predicate but the most essential, necessary and universal function of existence: the function which allows each thing to be itself, to be one and the same. The principle of Being-in is that which freely grants each thing the permission to *be*, to rest and recollect itself from the movement of becoming.

Kearney: Do you see this Greek metaphysics of relation radicalizing our understanding of the Judeo-Christian tradition?

Breton: I believe that both metaphysical relations—the Being-towards and the Being-in—are equally essential for an understanding of Judeo-Christian theology. At this level, I see no great opposition between Greek and Biblical thought. What we call the historical "meaning" of Christianity or Judaism is the tradition of interpretations that have been historically ascribed to them; and in the history of Western thinking these interpretations are inextricably related to Hellenic concepts of ontology. Between the two traditions—the Greek and the Biblical—there is a creative tension which ensures that we are never fully at our intellectual ease in either. We are inevitably committed to this philosophical exodus, this vacillation between two "homes" of thought. We have left the home of Israel just as we have left the home of Greece. We remain homesick for both. We cannot renounce the intellectual nostalgia of this double allegiance. The Western thinker is divided from *within*.

Kearney: Do you see Thomism as an attempt to bridge these two traditions in your own thought?

Breton: I consider Thomism to be the paleoancephalus of my philosophical formation. There were three areas in the work of St. Thomas which particularly preoccupied me: (1) the attempt to think God and Being together; (2) the theory of intentionality and formal objects—which I rediscovered later in Brentano and Husserl (I was especially impressed by Thomas's statement that relation consists of a certain transit or transitivity; this implies that Being is transitive and that our entire existence is a series of transitions towards the other, the loving potency which forever searches for its fulfillment in act); (3) the Thomistic definition of freedom or the free being as the being that is "cause of itself" (*causa sui*). This third concept occupied a very important place in my thought. For something to be free thus meant that, as cause of itself, it can create something new, almost from nothing. For the thinker it offers the free possibility to open up new paths of enquiry not already charted or inscribed in the map of the world.

Kearney: How did you find your way from Thomism to phenomenology?

Breton: Like most philosophers of my generation I was deeply influenced by the phenomenological movement inaugurated by Husserl and his disciples, Ingarden, Häring, Heidegger and so on. I saw the phenomenological emphasis on intentionality—the methodological investigation of how our consciousness is always intentionally directed towards something *beyond* itself—as a mean of extending three of my primary intellectual concerns: (1) the logic of relations governing the activity of the human mind; (2) the dynamic teleological aspect of Thomistic metaphysics expressed in the notion of the *esse ad;* and (3) the Biblical concept of exodus. Of course, the original contribution of Husserlian phenomenology was to delineate and describe the relation of intentionality in terms of concrete experience—our everyday being-in-the-world, to ground our logical and metaphysical concepts in the lived experience of consciousness. Later, particularly in a work like *Etre, monde, imaginaire,* I tried to combine these Husserlian insights into a philosophy of intentional relations invoking a more poetic language of metaphor and metamorphosis. My aim here was to suggest how our being-in-the-world, and our understanding of this being, unfolds as a creative interplay between the *logos* of reason, which unifies, regulates, structures, and the *mythos* of poetry, symbol and myth, which is forever transcending and revising the order of *logos*. Both of these directions of consciousness—the positing power of *logos* and the differentiating power of *mythos*—are founded on an *imaginaire-rien* which I define as the universal principle of language, a superabundant play which engenders all meanings.

Kearney: What would you describe as the specifically phenomenological characteristics of your work, given your early fascination for the Husserlian notion of phenomenology?

Breton: First, I would say it was through my interest in the "metaphysics of relation" that I became interested (via Brentano, on whom I was working in my Rome lectures) in Husserlian phenomenology. In fact, the relation of intentionality, which Brentano had retrieved from medieval scholasticism and "reactivated" for contemporary philosophical purposes, struck me as offering a very liberating understanding of meaning, irreducible both to the strictly "logical" notion of relations current in the forties and fifties, and to the traditional ontological notion of the "transcendental" rapports between matter and form, essence and existence, and more generally between potency and act (rapports which I preferred to call "structural" and which were typically articulated in Hamelin's *Eléments principaux de la représentation*). In my early work *Conscience et intentionalité*, I had already projected an enlarged notion of intentionality and I well remember a discussion with Jean Beaufret (one of the first advocates of existentialist and Heideggerian phenomenology in France) in which I engaged him on the crucial question of the transition from intentionality to "existence": a question which, it seemed to me, represented a new and deeper understanding of the concept of the *esse ad* which was to pursue me all of my life. My initial interest in phenomenology, which corresponded therefore to my keenest philosophical preoccupations, also extended to my later works, in particular *Approches phénoménologiques de l'idée d'être* and *Etre, monde, imaginare*. Overall I would say that the most inspiring aspect of phenomenology for me was its emphasis on the *prepredicative* and prereflective dimensions of experience. Indeed it was with this precise emphasis in mind that I distinguished in *Conscience et intentionalité* between several stratifications of consciousness: intentionality as a psychological act; intentionality as a "potency/

power" (*puissance*) relating to formal objects; and a transcendental intentionality representing the opening of the soul to *Being as Being*. It is along similar lines that, in the first part of *Etre, monde, imaginaire,* I proposed an analysis of what is meant by the "language of being" in a less rudimentary way than that proposed by scholasticism or Thomism. I must admit, however, that in my early studies in phenomenology I paid little attention to the celebrated phenomenological reduction which, in the fifties, tormented those philosophers of my generation inspired by the Husserlian "discovery." (It was only later, by means of my reflections on freedom, that I came to appreciate somewhat what was involved in the reduction.) In summary, I would say that for me phenomenology was an extraordinary stimulant to my thinking, serving to crystallize some of my most formative philosophical concerns and ultimately providing me with an effective method of analyzing the key notions of "passage," and "transit" which the metaphysics of relation first impressed upon me.

Kearney: Another of your recent works, *The Theory of Ideologies,* also seems to be a variation on this theme of creative intentionality or transcendence. I'm thinking particularly of the key term of this work—the "operator of transcendence."

Breton: This recent critique of ideology sprang from my fundamental preoccupation with the question of the "zero." The zero is a conceptual or mathematical way of formulating the metaphysical idea of the quasi-nothing (*rien*), or the Christian notion of the Cross—the emptiness of the crypt where Christian thinking as a critical thinking takes its source. A genuine questioning of ideology requires such a critical distance or dis-position. Without it, one can easily be misled by dogmatic ideologies—be they political or philosophical, or ecclesiastical.

The neoplatonists also taught the importance of keeping a distance from all categories of facile objectivization. Their very definition of Being as *Eidos* or Form expresses this critical reserve. They realized that our philosophical categories are really *figures* of thought, and are thus capable of being critically altered or transcended towards the truth of the One which is beyond all the forms and figures of established ontology. So that when the neoplatonists spoke of the One or God, they spoke of it in terms of critical reserve or qualification: *hos* or *oion, quasi* or *quatenus*—God *as* this or that ontological form. In short, since the Divine One was considered to be "beyond being," He could only be thought of *as* being, or *as if* He were being. One could not say: God *is* being. The critical notion of the quasi-nothing, functioning as the "operator of transcendence," thus prevented God from being reduced to a simplified or idolatrous ontology.

This neoplatonic notion of critical distance is confirmed by the Christian notion of mystery—and particularly the practice of mystical speculation advanced by Eckhart and other Christian mystics who remained very suspicious of all ontological objectivizations of God. The model of reason demanded by metaphysical thinking must, I believe, be accompanied by a mystical appreciation for that which remains beyond the reach of this metaphysical model. This is why I always felt the need to balance the Greek fidelity to Being with Biblical fidelity to the exodus—particularly as expressed in the Christian theology of the Passion and the Cross.

Kearney: Could you explain in more detail how your theological interpretation of the Passion as dispossession/disposition relates to the critique of contemporary ideologies? I think this is a crucial transition in your thinking and perhaps accounts for your occasional leanings towards the Marxist critique.

Breton: I believe that the Christian doctrine of dispossession can be translated into modern "socio-political" terms as a critique of power. There is a certain correspondence between the mystical—neoplatonic critique of the Divine attributes—as an attempt to *possess* God in terms of ontological properties which would reduce His transcendence to the immanence of Being—and the Marxist critique of private property. Christianity and authentic Marxism share a common call to dispossession and a critical detachment from the prevailing order. I was always struck by the similarities between the Christian doctrine of eschatological justice where Jesus identified with the poor—"I was naked. I was hungry. I was thirsty. I was imprisoned." (Matthew 10:9)—and the Marxist ideal of universal justice for the dispossessed. I think that this universal "I" of Christ—not to be confused with a transcendental or absolute Ego—which is enigmatically present in every poor or outcast person who has not yet been allowed the full humanity of justice, can find common cause with what is best in genuine Marxism. I am not saying that the two are the same. For while Christianity sponsors a categorical imperative for human justice and liberation (which certain brands of Marxism also endorse), it is not simply reducible to this imperative. While both share what Ernst Bloch called a common "principle of hope" (*principe-espérance*), pointing towards a utopian horizon in the future, Christianity transcends the limits of historical materialism in the name of a prophetic eschatology (i.e., the Coming of the Kingdom).

The term "Christian-Marxist" is a loaded and ambiguous one: it may serve as a *question*—with all the creative, thought-provoking tensions that genuine questioning implies—but not as a *solution*. We should remain cautious about invoking such terms uncritically as yet another ideological authority.

Kearney: How would you react to those who construe your recent work as a "Christian atheism"?

Breton: This is a dangerous term and I would not like to be thus characterized. To refuse the attempts to possess God by reducing Him to an ontological substance or political power— that is, an ideological weapon—is not to disbelieve in God; on the contrary, I would argue that it is a way of remaining faithful to one's belief. The critical refusal of ideological theism is not a refusal of God. It implies rather that the secondary definitions of God in terms of proposition (I believe *that* God exists) or predication (God *is* this or that) must be continually brought back to their primary origin in existential belief (I believe *in* God). This existential belief involves the believer in an intentional relation with God which is perhaps best described in terms of trust and transition. The move to institutionalize this belief in an invariant corpus of dogmas, doctrines and propositions was natural, perhaps even inevitable if Christianity was to survive the vagaries and contingencies of history. But this movement of *conservation* must always be accompanied by a *critical* counter-movement which reminds us that God cannot ultimately be objectified or immobilized in ontological or institutional (i.e., anthropomorphic) structures. In a recent study entitled *Théorie des idéologies et la réponse de la foi* I tried to reflect on this problem by discussing the central implications of the term *credo* in relation to the three movements of belief—existential, propositional and predicative—mentioned above. Religious faith begins with belief-in-God which expresses itself as an intentional being-towards-God. It involves the primary existential idioms of desire, enchantment and hope, etc. It is only subsequently that we return upon the existential level to appropriate the riches encountered in the immediacy of this original experience. Thus the second movement of faith takes place as an attempt to define and order the content and form of one's existential belief. It is as if one thus draws a golden circle around one's religious experience which one calls "tradition" or "heritage" or "doctrine" and affirms *that* God exists and that God is good and almighty, etc. In this way the vertical arrow of our primary intentional belief becomes a reflective or recollective circle—with those on the inside calling themselves Christian and those on the outside non-Christian. I think that this second move is indispensable in that every religion requires the form of a "society," and every society requires a specific identity and foundation. A religion that is content to be "anything at all" very easily becomes "nothing at all"—as indeterminate and all-inconclusive as the category of Being-as-Being. In the third movement, reflection goes beyond both the modalities of "I believe *in*" and "I believe *that*" to the definition of God as a *proposition in itself*: "God *is* this or that." Hence the intentional distance or commitment implied by the first two movements of "*I* believe" is transcended and dogmatic theology instantiates itself as a historical institution or organization. It is the duty of the religious or theistic thinker to serve such institutional belief by reminding it that its doctrines are not autonomous or eternally guaranteed but intellectual sedimentations of the original "I believe" wherein God reveals Himself to man. This critical exigency of faithfulness to the irreducible mystery and radicality of Divine revelation is beautifully expressed in a passage in Kings 1:2, where Elijah goes in search of God but discovers him not in the rocks, in the storm, in the shaking earth, nor in the fire, but in the voice of a gentle breeze as it passes through the mountain cave. God is passage not possession.

Kearney: Can this critique of theistic ideology also be applied to political ideologies which constitute the objectified or impersonalized institutions of contemporary society?

Breton: I think so. But we must remember the natural and almost inevitable reasons for the emergence of ideologies. Ideology springs from the fact that there is an ontological rupture between existence and consciousness. We do not coincide with ourselves. We exist before we are conscious of our existence; and this means that our reflective consciousness is always to some extent out of joint with the existential conditions that fostered it. Freud realized this when he spoke about the gap between the conscious and the unconscious. I would say that every form of *thought* is ideology to the extent that it does not and cannot fully coincide with the *being* of which it is the thought. The existence of ideologies reminds us that there is a margin of obscurity which we can never completely recuperate or remove. The pure identification of Being and Thought—i.e., the Thought that thinks itself as Being/Being as the Self-Thinking-Thought—is the Aristotelian-Thomistic definition of Divine self-understanding that no ideology can legitimately pretend to emulate. Human thought can never be perfectly transparent or adequate to itself. It is the role of the philosopher to challenge all ideological claims to such absolute knowledge and, by implication, to absolute power.

Kearney: You once stated: "The cross of my faith, will it not remain this interrogation mark which ancient legend tells us is the first-born of all creation?" If your philosophy does remain this critical interrogation mark, can it ever serve as a creative affirmation? Is it not inevitably condemned to a *via negativa*?

Breton: The two aspects of philosophy—as negation and affirmation—are for me by no means incompatible. Though the critical aspect is more in evidence in contemporary thinking, including my own, I would insist that the first step in philosophy—and therefore its *sine qua non*—is a fundamental experience of wonder, curiosity, or enchantment: in short *affirmation.* My enthusiasm for philosophy began in the same way as my enthusiasm for poetry or the Bible, by *responding* to texts that sang to me. Writing retraces those paths that sing to us (*chantent*) and thus enchant (*enchantent*) us. In this sense, I see a close relationship between philosophy, theology and poetics. Philosophy never speaks to us in the abstract with a capital *P;* but in the engaging terms of certain chosen texts (*morceaux choisis*)—in my own case, certain texts of the pre-Socratics, Aristotle, Plato, the neoplatonists or St. Thomas, Schelling, Husserl and Heidegger. The desire to know philosophy as a totality—the Hegelian temptation to absolute knowledge—is not only dangerous but impossible; one can never reduce the infinite richness of our existential experience to the totalizing limits of Reason.

Kearney: But would you not acknowledge essential differences between philosophy and poetry as modes of this *affirmation enchantée?*

Breton: The main difference between philosophy and poetry as I see it is that while both originate in an experience of enchantment which draws us and commits us to the world, philosophy is obliged, in a second movement, to critically transcend and interrogate the world, both as life-experience and poetic-experience. Philosophy thus leads a double life of residing within and without the world. Perhaps one of the greatest enigmas of philosophy is that a thinking being can serve as a chain in the historical world and yet also break free from this chain, rise above it (partially at least) in order to question its ultimate origin and meaning. Poetry celebrates *that* the world exists; philosophy asks *why* the world exists. Schelling and Husserl implicitly acknowledged this distinction when they spoke of the philosophical need to go beyond or suspend the natural attitude (which would include our primary poetic experience), in which all thinking begins, to a transcendental or questioning attitude:

to be *in* the world and yet not *of* the world, to be *inside* and *outside* at once.

Kearney: How do you see this double fidelity to the philosophical and poetic attitudes operating in your own work?

Breton: My work operates on the basis of two overriding impulses or passions. On the one hand, it strives for scientific rigor and form—a striving epitomized by my preoccupation with the mathematical logic of relations and the search for the principle of reason. On the other hand, I began to wonder if this search for rigor and reason might not ultimately lead to the sterile tautologies of a *mathesis universalis:* the pretentious claim to possess an absolutely certain Principle-Foundation through a synthesis of Aristotelian logic, Euclidean geometry and the Scholastic doctrine of Transcendentals. And this doubt provided a space for the emergence of a second fundamental passion— what I might call my "poetic inclination." This second poetic passion challenged the speculative claim to absolute identity or totality and revived an attentiveness to the vibrant multiplicity of the lifeworld. I suppose this poetic inclination can be witnessed, in its modernist guise, in Mallarmé's notion of "dissemination." I chose the terms "metaphor" and "metamorphosis" to express this reality of movement, alteration and diversification. And Derrida, Lyotard, Deleuze and Lévinas have developed their respective philosophies of "difference," repudiating the principle of identity for either the subject or the object. It is my own conviction that the classical metaphysics of identity and the modernist poetics of difference need each other, for both correspond to fundamental impulses in human thinking. This is what I tried to express in *Etre, monde, imaginaire* when I analyzed how the speculative principle of the *Logos* and the poetic principle of the *Mythos* are committed to each other in a creative conflict which unfolds in the free space of the *imaginaire.* This act of faith in the "imaginary," in the open horizon of the possible where oppositions confront and recreate each other, is where my initial reflections on the *Esse-in* and the *Esse-ad* have led me.

I might summarize this dual allegiance of my work as follows.

To consider philosophy as an exclusively critical or speculative movement is to condemn it to an endless contestation which can easily slip into the nihilism of a *reductio ad absurdum*. Philosophy must continually remind itself of its origins in the bedrock of real experience. Only when one has experienced the opaque profundity of existential or religious reality can one legitimately take one's critical distance in order to question or reflect upon it. Similarly, it is only when one has been immersed in the social lifeworld that one can begin to interrogate the ideological structures which regulate it. Philosophy always presupposes the ability to say: *this* is what a tree is, *this* is how authority works, *this* is what a tribunal consists of, etc. The speculative instance is inextricably dependent upon the concrete immediacy of the person's lived experience. It cannot afford to ignore the existential conditions which precede it. I have always been struck by Suarez's principle of identity, which states that "every being has an essence which constitutes and determines it." Philosophy begins with a commitment to the determining world and only in an ulterior, reflexive moment proceeds to "objectify" or "formalize." Philosophy does not begin with Kant— though the "critical" turn is a crucial stage in its development. I think we should be grateful to Marx for having turned idealism on its head and for making it more humble towards reality; only by being engaged to the living body of history can critical thinking avoid becoming a corpse of solipsistic introspection. It is because philosophy is both *critique* and *commitment* that it can distance itself from the world precisely in order to transform it.

Kearney: This summary analysis of your philosophy reminds me of your theological interpretation of the ecumenical dialectic between Catholic, Protestant and Orthodox thinking in *La Foi et raison logique*.

Breton: In this work I tried to rethink ecumenism in terms of a group of metaphysical operations. In this schema, the Catholic tradition privileged the operation of transitivity and transformation, functioning as a process of historical realism bound to the preservation of Revelation in the temporal world. The Protestant Reform privileged the operation of a critical conversion (turning around) which returned to the fundamental origins of Christianity. And thirdly, the Orthodox church of oriental Christianity privileged the operation of "manence" (*Esse-in*) or indwelling. I argued that all three movements—of historical transformation, critical return and spiritual dwelling—are essential to the Christian reality, ensuring that it remains transitive and intransitive, transcendent and immanent. The history of Christianity is the drama of this divergence and belonging-together of Catholicism, Protestantism and Orthodoxy as a fecund tension between complementary differences. I think that ecumenism is facile if it ignores the importance of this creative tension. It is only when one assumes the specificity of one's own religious tradition (in my case Catholic) that one can fully appreciate the *other*—the essential contribution which the other traditions make to one's own.

Kearney: France produced a considerable number of "Christian philosophers" in the first half of this century, including Marcel, Mounier, Maritain and Gilson. Would you consider yourself a Christian philosopher?

Breton: I am a Christian philosopher to the extent that the primary experience that fostered and colored much of my philosophical thinking was, as I explained at the outset, specifically Christian in certain respects—particularly as it determined my reflections on the Passion and the Cross. Such Christian reflection frequently dovetailed with my preoccupation with Greek and neoplatonic thought. For example, my description of the Cross as the "seed of non-being" (*german nihili*) bears an intimate correspondence to Proclus's notion of the *sperma meontos*. The neoplatonic attempts to critically radicalize the Platonic philosophy of Being (*On*) find common ground here with the theology of the Cross. If the theology of Glory—with its splendid doctrine of the superabundance of grace—is divorced from the critical theology of the Cross, it can degenerate into triumphalism. Grace is not power but dispossession because it is given under the interrogative sign of the Cross. To the extent, therefore, that the theology of the Cross deeply affected my whole attitude to thought, I would be prepared to consider myself a "Christian" philosopher. But I would insist that philosophy and theology are separate, if equally valid, disciplines of thought. Whereas the theologian can presuppose the Christian tradition as a series of Revealed doctrines, the philosopher—even the Christian philosopher—cannot. The theologian believes truth is given, the philosopher goes in search of it.

SELECT BIBLIOGRAPHY OF STANISLAS BRETON

L'Esse in *et l'esse* ad *dans la métaphysique de la relation*, Rome, 1951.

La Passion du Christ et les philosophies, Eco, Terramo, 1954.

Conscience et intentionalité, Vitte, Paris-Lyon, 1956.

Approches phénoménologiques de l'idée d'être, Vitte, Paris-Lyon, 1959.

Situation de la philosophie contemporaine, Vitte, Paris-Lyon, 1959.

Essence et existence, P.U.F., Paris, 1962.

Le Problème de l'être spirituel dans la philosophie de N. Hartman, Vitte, Paris-Lyon, 1962.

Mystique de la Passion, Desclée, Tournai, 1962.

Saint Thomas d'Aquin, Seghers, Paris, 1965.

Philosophie et mathématiques chez Proclus, Beauchesne, Paris, 1969.

Du principe, coéd, Aubier, Cerf, Desclée, Delachaux, Paris, 1971.

La Foi et raison logique, Le Seuil, Paris, 1971.

Etre, monde, imaginaire, Le Seuil, Paris, 1976.

Théorie des idéologies, Desclée, Paris, 1976.

Spinoza, Théologie et politique, Desclée, Paris, 1977.

INDEX

Hymn, 1
Hypostasis, xiii
Hypostatic union, 91, 92, 97

Ibn Arabi, 94
Idea, 31
Idealism, x
Identity, 81; Christian, 109, 111; and distinction, 101, 102
Ideology, 53, 55; critique of ideologies, 136, 139; justification of, 110; need for theory of, xviii
Il Poverello, 39. *See also* Francis of Assisi
"Imaginary nothing"*(imaginaire rien),* xvii, xxvii, 134
Imagination, 39
Incarnation, 111, 130
Indisposability, 18, 20, 24, 26, 29
Indisposable, the, 24–29, 57
Indwelling, xxiv
Ineffable, xvi, xxvi, 37; ineffability, 74
Infirmity, 7, 9, 14, 15, 18, 26, 52, 56, 64, 83, 73, 108
Ingarden, 133
Insecurity, 20
Institut Catholique, xii
"Intellectual love of God." *See* Love
Intelligence, 14, 31
Intentionality, x, 64–65, 133
Interrogation, mark of, 42, 50, 102, 128, 139, 143
Involuntary *(non-vouloir),* xvii
Irreversibility of death, 128
Islam, 90
Israel and Greece, xxiii, 109. *See also* Athens: and Jerusalem; Greek and Jew

Jerusalem, xxii. *See also* Athens: and Jerusalem
Jesus, 37, 87, 191. *See also* Christ
Jew-Greek, xxii, 4–5, 73, 97. *See also* Greek and Jew; Greece and Israel; Athens: and Jerusalem
Johannine: Logos, 100–115; Prologue, 100; Word, xix, 45, 119
John, 22, 100–103
John the Baptist, 103
Judaism, rupture with, 26
Judgment, 7, 9, 13, 20, 41, 43–44, 51, 54, 73, 76, 78, 80; of the Cross, xxiv, xxvi, 116, 112, 127; "determining" and "reflective," 112–15; of freedom, 102; Last judgment, 122, 126; and the Sign of Contradiction, 7; of uselessness, 124; of the Word of the Cross, 115, 120
Justice, 10, 25, 55–58, 61, 79, 136–37
Just One, the, 54

Kant, Immanuel, xviii, 108; judgment, 112; Kantian Dialectic, 106
Kenosis, xix, xxiv; interpretations of, 83–99, 111, 122, 127
Kenotic, 84
Kernel/kerygmatic, 22; evangelical, 55
Kerygma, 24, 47, 41, 48–49, 51, 61, 64, 73; of the Cross, 110
Kingdom, coming of on earth, 124
Knowledge of the deity, xxi
Krisis, 54

Lallement, Daniel, xii
Language, viii, xx, xxiii, xxv–xxvi,